HART'S RULES

HART'S RULES

FOR COMPOSITORS
AND READERS
AT THE
UNIVERSITY PRESS
OXFORD

Thirty-ninth edition
Completely revised

OXFORD UNIVERSITY PRESS

OXFORD   NEW YORK

Oxford University Press, Walton Street, Oxford OX2 6DP

Oxford New York Toronto
Delhi Bombay Calcutta Madras Karachi
Petaling Jaya Singapore Hong Kong Tokyo
Nairobi Dar es Salaam Cape Town
Melbourne Auckland

and associated companies in
Berlin Ibadan

Originally compiled by Horace Hart, MA Printer to the University,
1883–1915. First edition, 1893. Fifteenth edition (the first for general
sale), 1904. Thirty-eighth edition, 1978. Thirty-ninth edition, 1983.

This edition first published 1983
Reprinted 1984, 1986 (with corrections),
1987 (with corrections), 1989 (with corrections)

British Library Cataloguing in Publication Data

Hart, Horace
Hart's rules for compositors and readers at the
University Press, Oxford.—39th ed.
1. Type-setting
I. Title
686.2'25   Z253
ISBN 0-19-212983-X

Printed in Great Britain
at the University Printing House, Oxford
by David Stanford
Printer to the University

PREFACE TO THE
THIRTY-NINTH EDITION

WITH the replacing of Collins, *Authors and Printers Dictionary*, by the new *Oxford Dictionary for Writers and Editors*, it was almost inevitable that another edition of this little book would follow. It has been revised and updated and all word-lists brought into line generally with *ODWE*. Many users will have both books on their shelves; no doubt it will be appreciated that one may always be slightly ahead of the other in some way.

The swiftly changing face of the industry is reflected in a new section (in the Appendix) on Machine Readable Codes, whilst the multiplicity of new setting systems has meant taking a seemingly backwards step. In the previous edition values for spacing were based on the Monotype 18-unit system. Now it has been decided, in the interest of clarity, to reintroduce older terms and give to each a percentage-value related to the em-space (see p. xi).

Recent editions of *Hart's Rules* have seen the gradual expansion of the Foreign Languages section. This, the 39th (reset) edition, carries on this tradition by including a valuable (if overdue) guide to the setting of Welsh, and of Dutch and Afrikaans.

Once more I must point out that the revision of this publication is the work of several people, and I should like to draw attention to the valuable help given by the Oxford Dictionaries staff. A special word of thanks is due to Harold Boyce, who has carried the main burden of responsibility for editions and revisions during the last twenty-five years while he was Head Reader here.   E.B.

PREFACE

(1914)

IT is quite clearly set out on the title-page in previous editions of these Rules and Examples, that they were intended especially *for Compositors and Readers at the Clarendon Press*. Consequently it seems necessary to explain why an edition or impression is now offered to so much of the General Public as is interested in the technicalities of Typography, or wishes to be guided to a choice amidst alternative spellings.

On the production of the First Edition at the Oxford Press, copies were placed at the disposal of all Readers, Compositors, and Compositor-apprentices; and other copies found their way into the possession of Authors and Editors of books then in the printers' hands. Subsequently, friends of authors, and readers and compositors in other printing-offices, began to ask for copies, which were always supplied without charge. By and by applications for copies were received from persons who had no absolute claim to be supplied gratuitously; but, as many of such requests came from Officials of the King's Government at Home, in the Colonies, and in India, it was thought advisable, on the whole, to continue the practice of presentation.

Recently, however, it became known that copies of the booklet were *on sale* in London. A correspondent wrote that he had just bought a copy 'at the Stores'; and as it seems more than complaisant to provide gratuitously what may afterwards be sold for profit, there is no alternative but to publish this little book.

As to the origin and progress of the work, it was begun in 1864, when the compiler was a member of

the London Association of Correctors of the Press.
With the assistance of a small band of fellow members employed in the same printing-office as himself,
a first list of examples was drawn up, to furnish
a working basis.

Fate so ordained that, in course of years, the
writer became in succession general manager of
three London printing-houses. In each of these
institutions additions were made to his selected list
of words, which, in this way, gradually expanded—
embodying what compositors term 'the Rule of the
House'.

In 1883, as Controller of the Oxford Press, the
compiler began afresh the work of adaptation; but
pressure of other duties deferred its completion
nearly ten years, for the first edition is dated 1893.
Even at that date the book lacked the seal of final
approval, being only part of a system of printing-
office management.

In due course, Sir J. A. H. Murray and Dr
Henry Bradley, editors of the *Oxford Dictionary*,
were kind enough to revise and approve all the
English spellings. Bearing the stamp of their sanc-
tion, the booklet has an authority which it could not
otherwise have claimed.

To subsequent editions the late Professor Robinson Ellis and Mr H. Stuart Jones contributed two
appendixes, containing instructions for the Division
of Words in Latin and Greek; and the section on the
German Language was revised by Dr Karl Breul,
Reader in Germanic in the University of Cambridge.

Recent issues of this work comprise many additions and some rearrangement. The compiler has
encouraged the proof-readers of the University
Press from time to time to keep memoranda of
troublesome words in frequent—or indeed in occasional—use, not recorded in previous issues of the
'Rules', and to make notes of the mode of printing

them which is decided on. As each edition of the book becomes exhausted such words are reconsidered, and in their approved form are incorporated into the pages of the forthcoming edition. The same remark applies to new words which appear unexpectedly, like new planets, and take their place in what Sir James Murray calls the 'World of Words'. Such instances as airman, airship, sabotage, seaplane, stepney-wheel, syndicalism, will occur to every newspaper reader.

Lastly, it ought to be added that in one or two cases a particular way of spelling a word or punctuating a sentence has been completely changed. This does not often mean that an error has been discovered in the 'Rules'; but rather that the fashion has altered, and that it is necessary to guide the compositor accordingly.   H.H.

CONTENTS

RULES FOR SETTING
FOREIGN LANGUAGES

These rules apply generally. They are to be departed from only when authors require their own spelling and punctuation to be strictly adhered to, or when other exceptions are given in writing.

SPACING TERMS: DEFINITIONS

THE following definitions will apply throughout this book. The figures refer to the 96-unit system predominantly in use at the University Press.

LINEAR SPACES: Fixed values specified at the outset of the job by editor, printer, or designer:

$$
\begin{aligned}
\text{Em quad} &= 96 \text{ units} \\
\text{En quad} &= 48 \text{ units} \\
\text{Thick space} &= 32 \text{ units} \\
\text{Middle space} &= 24 \text{ units} \\
\text{Thin space} &= 19 \text{ units} \\
\text{One point} &= 8 \text{ units} \\
\text{Half point} &= 4 \text{ units} \\
\text{Quarter point} &= 2 \text{ units.}
\end{aligned}
$$

This system is applicable to each typeface size, so that the actual value in space terms varies with the size of type employed, i.e. a 6 pt em is half a 12 pt em; but each is divisible into 96 units.

INTERLINEAR SPACES: Where necessary the expressions used, especially in the Appendix, should be converted at the copy-preparation stage, and in consultation with the designer, from point values to millimetres.

RULES FOR SETTING ENGLISH

A or AN

(*a*) Before all normal vowels and diphthongs: *an*

an actor	an eagle	an instance
an ailment	an exit	an opening
an author	an iambic	an uncle

(*b*) Before a syllable beginning with a vowel but with the sound of *w*- or *y*-: *a*

a eulogy	a once-only	a unique
a ewe	a one	a use

(*c*) Before aspirated *h*: *a*

a harvest	a hero	a home
a height	a hill	a hoop
a help	a hire	a huge

This applies equally to words in which the first syllable is unstressed:

a habitual	a heretical	a historical
a heraldic	a heroic	a hypothesis

However, old usage supports the use of *an* in such cases (also 'an humble'), and this may be adopted where it is necessary to follow a particular writer's individual style.

In some words initial *h* may be either aspirated or silent. The following are recommended in the absence of any preference of the author's:

a *habitué*	a hotel

(*d*) Before silent *h*: *an*

an heir	an hour
an honour	

(*e*) Before all normal consonants: *a*

(*f*) With single letters and groups of letters *pronounced as letters*, be guided by pronunciation:

a B road	a KLM flight
a CMS missionary	a TUC leader

but

an A road	an MCC ruling
an FA cup match	an OUP book
an IOU	an RAC badge

assuming that these will not be expanded by the reader and pronounced 'a Football Association cup match', etc.

If pronounced with a consonantal sound, however, initials must be preceded by *a*:

a NATO conference (pronounced 'nato')

a MS (usually pronounced 'manuscript' not 'em-ess')

ABBREVIATIONS AND CONTRACTIONS

As a general rule, abbreviations and contractions should be followed by a full point unless the shortened form consists of upper-case initials *or* is a recognized acronym pronounced as a single word: thus print BBC, HMS, OUP, PAYE, PLC, SDP, SPCK, TUC, WEA; Anzac, Aslib, Fiat, Naafi (or NAAFI).

Abbreviations and contractions consisting of a mixture of upper and lower case take full points, as in I.o.W. (Isle of Wight), Bt. (Baronet), Kt. (Knight), Ltd. (Limited), St. (Street), and University degrees (D.Litt., D.Phil., Ph.D., etc.); exceptions to be made for Dr (Doctor), Revd (Reverend: *not* Rev), Mr, Mrs, Mme, Mlle, St (Saint); here full points are not required.

Abbreviations and contractions used after names, such as Bt., Esq., Jun., SJ, etc., should be preceded by a comma.

When necessary, the names of days and months to be shown as below:

Sun. Mon. Tue. Wed. Thur. Fri. Sat.

Jan. Feb. Mar. Apr. May June
July Aug. Sept. Oct. Nov. Dec.

Where the name of a county is abbreviated, as Yorks., Cambs., Berks., use a full point; but print Hants (no full point) because it is not a modern abbreviation.

4to, 8vo, 12mo, etc. (sizes of books), are symbols, and should not have full points. A parallel case is that of 1st, 2nd, 3rd, and so on.

In non-technical work print lb. and oz. for both sing. and pl.; not lbs. or ozs. Also omit the plural -s in the following: bu., cm., cwt., dwt., g. (= grams), gr. (= grains), in., min., mm., sec. Insert the plural -s in hrs., qrs., yds. (In technical work BS 1991 should be followed: see p. 57.)

Print £44. 1s. 4d., but £44 1s. 4d. in tabular matter (for decimal currency see p. 87).

When beginning a footnote, c. [*circa*], e.g., i.e., l. or ll., l.c., p. or pp., to be in lower case.

Print a.m., p.m., in lower case.

Generally print etc. *not* &c. Use the ampersand in names of firms, as Freeman, Hardy, & Willis. The ampersand may be used, as directed, in dictionary or similar work.

The points of the compass, N. S. E. W., when separately used, to have a full point: but print NE, NNW, etc. These letters to be used only in geographical or similar matter: do not, even if N. is in the copy, use the abbreviation in ordinary narrative; print 'Woodstock is eight miles north of Carfax'.

MS = manuscript, MSS = manuscripts, to be spelt out when used in a general sense. But in works in which the abbreviations are frequently used (such as Introductions, Commentaries, etc., dealing with classical texts and technical in character), and in references to particular manuscripts, the contracted forms should be printed; e.g. the Worcester MS, the Harleian MSS, Add. MS 25642.

Print AS (Anglo-Saxon), ME (Middle English), OE (Old English), OHG (Old High German), and other similar combinations in philological works; but when an author prefers A.S., M.E., etc., no space should be put between the letters.

Print *OED* (*Oxford English Dictionary*), *DNB* (*Dictionary of National Biography*), *COD* (*Concise Oxford Dictionary*), EETS, os/es (Early English Text Society, Original Series/Extra Series), NEB (New English Bible).

For Saint use St generally, but S. if this is the author's consistent preference (plural SS). Before a French name use S. (masc., with point) or Ste (fem., no point).

Omit the apostrophe in the plurals B.Litt.s, MAs, MPs, QCs, the sixties, the 1960s.

Print A-bomb, H-bomb (no points).

Print UN (= United Nations), *not* UNO.

Print ITV, TV (no points).

Print C (Celsius or centigrade), F (Fahrenheit) without points.

As a rule, print nineteenth century, *not* 19th cent.; 9 per cent, *not* 9% (but 9‰ *not* per mille).

For Fig., No., Pl. see p. 12.

These rules may be altered to accord with an author's special wishes, providing usage is consistent throughout a given work; and it may be preferable to omit full points from shortened forms which appear with great frequency in a particular work. In addition common abbreviations and contractions may appear, as directed, without points in display work.

ABBREVIATIONS USED IN THE METRIC SYSTEM

For abbreviations of units see p. 3 (non-technical work), pp. 57–9 (scientific work).

BOOKS OF THE BIBLE

Names of the books of the Bible should be abbreviated as follows:

Old Testament

Gen.	1 Kgs.	Eccles.	Obad.
Exod.	2 Kgs.	S. of S.	Jonah
Lev.	1 Chr.	Isa.	Mic.
Num.	2 Chr.	Jer.	Nahum
Deut.	Ezra	Lam.	Hab.
Josh.	Neh.	Ezek.	Zeph.
Judg.	Esther	Dan.	Hag.
Ruth	Job	Hos.	Zech.
1 Sam.	Ps. (*pl.* Pss.)	Joel	Mal.
2 Sam.	Prov.	Amos	

New Testament

Matt.	2 Cor.	1 Tim.	2 Pet.
Mark	Gal.	2 Tim.	1 John
Luke	Eph.	Titus	2 John
John	Phil.	Philem.	3 John
Acts	Col.	Heb.	Jude
Rom.	1 Thess.	Jas.	Rev.
1 Cor.	2 Thess.	1 Pet.	

Apocrypha

1 Esd.	Wisd.	Bel & Dr.
2 Esd.	Ecclus. [= Sir.]	Pr. of Man.
Tobit	Baruch	1 Macc.
Judith	S. of III Ch.	2 Macc.
Rest of Esth.	Sus.	

There are also the extra-short forms Gn., Ex., Lv., Nu., Dt., etc. (OT), and Mt., Mk., Lk., Jn. (NT)—legitimate in narrow measure or marginal references.

BIOLOGICAL NOMENCLATURE

THE Latin name of a plant or an animal species usually consists of a binominal containing the name of a genus followed by a specific epithet or a specific name. Both parts should be printed in italic, with the generic name given an initial capital, e.g. *Primula vulgaris* (primrose), *Equus caballus* (horse). After the first mention of a species, when the name is given in full, later references may be shortened, if there is no risk of confusion, by the abbreviation of the generic name to its initial capital alone, followed by a full point: *P. vulgaris*, *E. caballus*. The generic name is sometimes used alone in reference to the genus as a whole and not a specific member of it. It may then be printed in roman without an initial capital when it is also the common name of the organism concerned, e.g. rhododendron, dahlia, tradescantia. Specific epithets are never used alone, except in the rare cases where they have become popular names; then they are printed in roman, e.g. japonica.

Names of animal subspecies have a third term added to the binominal, e.g. *Troglodytes troglodytes troglodytes* (wren). With plants, categories below the species level also have a third term added to their names, but only after an abbreviated form of a word indicating their rank, which is printed in roman. *Salix repens* var. *fusca* indicates a variety of the creeping willow, *Myrtus communis* subsp. *tarentina* a subspecies of the common myrtle.

Names of hybrid plants are indicated by a multiplication sign: *Cytisus* × *kewensis*. The names attached to cultivated varieties of plants should follow the binominal, printed in roman within single quotation marks: *Rosa wichuraiana* 'Dorothy Perkins'. The cultivar name may be preceded by the abbreviation cv., in which case the quotation marks are not used: *Rosa wichuraiana* cv. Dorothy Perkins.

Latin binominals or generic names alone may be followed by the surname of the person who published the first description of the organism concerned, using the name indicated. These surnames or abbreviations of them are called authorities and are printed in roman with initial capitals. *Primula vulgaris* Huds. shows that this name for the primrose was first used by William Hudson; *Homo sapiens* L. indicates that Linnaeus was the first to use this specific name for man.

Names of groups above the generic level—the main ones being orders, families, and tribes—are in the form of Latin plural nouns, to be printed in roman with initial capitals. The level of the taxon is usually indicated by the ending, e.g. the names of botanical or bacteriological families and orders end in -aceae and -ales; zoological families and sub-families are indicated by the endings -idae and -inae respectively. Ligatures should not be used in the printing of words of this form, or indeed in any biological nomenclature, with occasional exceptions such as the current *Supplement to the Oxford English Dictionary*, which follows the style established in the main *Oxford English Dictionary*, disregarding later changes.

Further guidance on the printing of Latin plant and animal names may be found in the International Codes of Botanical Nomenclature, Zoological Nomenclature, Nomenclature of Bacteriology, or Nomenclature of Cultivated Plants.

CAPITALS, SMALL CAPITALS, AND LOWER-CASE INITIALS

CAPITAL AND LOWER CASE

CAPITAL letters should be used for proper names: Smith is a baker; Baker is a smith.

They should be used also for:

(*a*) Prefixes and titles forming part of a compound name:

Sir Roger Tichborne, the Bishop of Oxford, the Duke of Wellington. [Note: in historical writing lower case is sometimes used, e.g. the duke of Normandy, the earl of Arundel. This should not be followed unless definitely prescribed as the style of the work or series.]

The King of England, the Prince of Wales—when the title of a particular person; but in a general sense lower case is correct: 'every king of England from William I to Richard II'; for 'king' is used here in a perfectly general sense, where 'monarch' or 'sovereign' would be equally correct.

(*b*) Parts of recognized geographical names:

Northern Ireland, i.e. the province, a political division; but 'northern England', a plain description in general terms. Similarly Western Australia, West Germany (officially the Federal Republic), East Germany (officially the German Democratic Republic), East Africa, West Africa, etc. Also New England (a recognized, though not political, division of USA); contrast 'a new England beyond the seas', which could be anywhere;

Firth of Clyde, Norfolk Broads, Straits of Gibraltar, Plymouth Sound, Thames Estuary (but estuary of the Thames);

Also River Plate (Río de la Plata), East River (New York), but the Thames, or the River Thames;

Topographical and urban names: planting wheat in the Fifty Acre, Trafalgar Square, Addison's Walk, London Road (if official name), but 'the London road' (that leading to London).

(*c*) Proper names of periods of time or natural phenomena, historical eras and events:

Palaeozoic era, Carboniferous, Tertiary, Old (New) Stone Age, Bronze Age, Iron Age. Also such terms as Chalcolithic, Early Minoan, Beaker Folk, etc., if these have a definite archaeological significance, as shown by the author's consistent usage;

Antiquity (occasionally used for Greek and Roman history), Classical, Byzantine, Dark Ages, Middle Ages, Renaissance (dark ages, middle ages, renaissance would be too general, but medieval (lower case) is accepted as referring specifically to the Middle Ages);

First World War, Second World War, etc., or World War I, II, if the copy is consistent.

(*d*) Proper names of institutions, movements, etc.:

Christianity, Marxism, Buddhism, Islam, the Church (when a proper name of the Christian Church as a whole, or of any institution called Church, e.g. (Roman) Catholic Church, Church of England; but lower case for the building, and for a church in a general sense, e.g. any church or sect).[1]

Church and State—both capitalized when viewed as comparable institutions, also 'the State' as a concept of political philosophy; the Crown, Parliament, Congress (US), House of Commons (of Representatives, US), House of Lords, Senate (when officially so called, but 'the House of Lords should

---

[1] In the New Testament, 'church' (*ekklesia*, otherwise translated 'congregation' or 'assembly') has lower case, as not yet a formal title.

be a senate composed of elder statesmen'), Treasury (British and US), Ministry of Finance, etc.

HM Government, or the Government, in official parlance and meaning a particular body of persons, the Ministers of the Crown and their staffs; but the government (lower case) is correct in general senses.

(*e*) Parties, denominations, and organizations, and their members:

Air Force, Army, Navy (as titles of particular organizations), Conservative, Labour, Liberal (in British politics); Socialist, Social Democrat, Christian Democrat (European countries, etc.); Republican, Democratic (USA); and so on. (But liberal, socialist, republican, democratic, etc., as normal adjectives when not party titles.)

Baptist, Congregationalist, Methodist, Presbyterian, Unitarian, Church of England, Anglican, Roman Catholic, Orthodox (i.e. Eastern Orthodox), Reformed, Evangelical (continental and US). (But congregational (singing, polity), reformed, unitarian views of God, orthodox belief, catholic sympathies in non-denominational sense.)[1]

Reformed, Puritan, etc., may be capitalized by particular authors or in particular contexts to make specific reference to the Reformation (sixteenth-seventeenth centuries in Europe) or Puritanism, as against reforming and puritan tendencies elsewhere, e.g. in monastic orders, non-Christian religions, etc.

The general rule is: capitalization makes a word more specific and limited in its reference: contrast a Christian scientist (man of science) and

---

[1] Note that the Church of Scotland is (since 1690) presbyterian in government, but the Church of England is episcopal; there exists also the Episcopal Church in Scotland. Only the *capitalized* terms are official titles: there are no such bodies as the Presbyterian Church of Scotland or the Episcopal Church of England.

a Christian Scientist (member of the Church of Christ Scientist).

(*f*) Titles of office-holders:

In certain cases and certain contexts these are virtually proper names of persons: HM the Queen, the Prime Minister, the Archbishop of Canterbury. The extension of this principle depends on the context: the President, e.g. of USA, of Magdalen College, Oxford, etc.

Similarly, the Bishop of Oxford, the Dean of Christ Church; and in a particular diocese, the Bishop, or within a particular cathedral or college, the Dean (referring to a particular individual, or at least a holder of a particular office: the Bishop is *ex officio* chairman of many committees). (But: when he became bishop, the bishops of the Church of England, appointment of bishops—such cases are better printed in lower case, and so with other office-holders.)

(*g*) Names of ships, aircraft types, railway engines, trade names, etc.:

The *Cutty Sark*, HMS *Dreadnought* (italic for ships' names, see also p. 24); the Königs, the fastest German battleships in 1916 (capitals but not italic for *types* of ships).

The Spitfire, the Flying Fortress, the Dakotas of the 1939–45 war. These are types, since aircraft do not usually have individual names; but 'the US bomber Enola Gay which dropped the atom bomb over Hiroshima on 6 August 1945' (not italic as not official like a ship's name).

A Viscount, an Elizabethan, a Concorde (airliners).

A Ford Cortina, a Vauxhall Astra (trade names). Aspro, Cow & Gate, Dreft, Persil, Tide, etc. Capitals must be used for proprietary names, which would sometimes be absurd with lower case, e.g. 'Mrs Jones washed with tide.'

Figure, Number, Plate (Fig., No., Pl.), should each begin with a capital, unless special instructions are given to the contrary.[1]

Pronouns referring to the Deity should begin with capitals only if so requested by the author: He, Him, His, Me, Mine, My, Thee, Thine, Thou; but even so print: who, whom, and whose. If the copy is not consistent or the author not insistent, lower case for all pronouns is much to be preferred, and as this follows the usage of the Bible and the Book of Common Prayer there is no real justification for capitals *as a rule*. They are now either old-fashioned or a personal preference of some (especially devotional) writers. (The Church of Scotland requires capitals in all its official publications.)

Words derived from proper names

adjectives:

(i) Use capital initial when usage favours it, and when connection with the proper name is still felt to be alive:

Christian, Dantesque, Hellenic, Homeric, Indian (elephant, tea), Machiavellian, Platonic (philosophy), Roman (Catholic, Empire), Shakespearian.

(ii) Use lower-case initial when connection with the proper name is remote or conventional:

arabic (letters), french (chalk, cricket, polish), italic (script), roman (numerals), and when the sense is an attribute or quality suggested by the proper name:

chauvinistic, gargantuan, herculean (feat, task), lilliputian, machiavellian (intrigue), platonic (love),

---

[1] See p. 3 for use of lower case for abbreviations at the beginning of a footnote.

protean, quixotic, titanic. (Usage favours a capital initial in certain less familiar cases, e.g. Draconian.)

verbs:

(i) Use capital initial when the sense of the verb is historical or cultural and has a direct reference to the proper name:

Americanize, Christianize, Europeanize, Hellenize, Latinize, Romanize.

(ii) Use lower-case initial when the sense is an activity associated with but not referring directly to the proper name:

bowdlerize, galvanize, macadamize, pasteurize.

nouns:

Use lower-case initial:

(i) When reference to the proper name is remote or allusive:

boycott, jersey (garment), mackintosh, morocco (leather), philippics, quisling, sandwich, suede, wellington (boot).

(ii) in names of scientific units:

ampere, joule, newton, volt, watt.

(iii) in names of metres:

alcaics, alexandrines, sapphics.

Biological nomenclature

For use of capitals and lower-case initials in biological nomenclature see pp. 6–7.

SMALL CAPITALS

For some abbreviations small capitals are usual. In printing these no space should be put between the letters:

AUC Anno urbis conditae

AD Anno Domini	AM Anno mundi
AH Anno Hegirae	BC Before Christ

a.m. (ante meridiem), p.m. (post meridiem), should be in lower case, except in lines of capitals or small capitals.

Text references to capital symbols in plates and line-blocks to be in small capitals, except in scientific work, where capitals are used.

DIVISION OF WORDS

Avoid divisions if at all possible, having regard for the requirements of typography (even spacing, etc.). Not to inconvenience the reader must always be one of the main considerations. The following rules and recommendations apply whenever possible: to avoid uneven spacing, however, one-syllable divisions of two letters are permissible (this should not be necessary in other than the narrowest measures).

Divide according to etymology, where this is obvious: atmo-sphere, bio-graphy, tele-phone, trans-port, un-equal. Otherwise divide according to *The Oxford Spelling Dictionary*:

abs-cess	em-brace	minis-ter
ab-stract	epis-copal	ob-scure
ana-lyse	estab-lish	origin-ally
appear-ance	Euro-pean	philo-sophy
celeb-rate	forget-ting	popu-lar
chil-dren	gener-ally	prim-ary
cor-respond-ence	haemor-rhage	prob-ably
depend-ent	illus-trate	prob-lem
de-scribe	immedi-ate	pun-ish
des-pise	import-ance	semb-lance
des-tiny	inexplic-able	thou-sand
dimin-ish	inter-pret	whist-ling
dis-connect	inter-est	

Do not divide two consonants which form one sound: calm-est, debt-ors, fea-ther (but post-humous), lamb-like (but lam-bent), laugh-able, poign-ant, tough-ish, wash-able, and ch when sounded as in ach-ing.

The endings -ism, -ist, -istic may be taken over, as: human-ism, botan-ist, character-istic; but note neo-logism, criti-cism (and so all words ending in -cism).

In present participles take over -ing, as: carry-ing, crown-ing, divid-ing, toll-ing; but chuck-ling, puzz-ling, rust-ling, trick-ling, and similar words.

The terminations -cial, -cian, -cious, -gious, -sion, -tial, -tion should not be divided when forming one sound, as in condescen-sion, espe-cially, forma-tion, Gre-cian, pugna-cious.

Words ending in -logy, -logist: archaeo-logy, etymo-logy, philo-logist, psycho-logist, tauto-logy are normally thus divided; but zoolo-gist.

Avoid divisions which might confuse or alter the meaning, the only permissible divisions of the following being: le-gends (not *leg-ends*), re-adjust (*read-just*), re-appear (*reap-pear*), an exact-ing (*ex-acting*) director, the old umbrella was re-covered and the lost one recovered (indivisible in this context).

Break hyphenated words at the hyphen (avoid introducing a second hyphen): counter-clockwise *not* counter-clock-wise. One-word compounds should be divided at the point of union: railway-man *not* rail-wayman. Divide between vowels only when they are sounded separately: cre-ate, but crea-ture.

Many compound scientific words, especially concerning anatomy, biology, and chemistry, are difficult when composition is not known. Divide at the hyphen if hyphenated—otherwise at the point of union. Generally one can divide after such forms as angio-, broncho-, cervico-, deutero-, dia-, glycero-, ophthalmo-, proto-, pseudo-; but note pseud-onym.

A divided word should not end a right-hand page, if it is possible to avoid it.

The divisions noted as preferable are not free from objection, and should be avoided when it is at all easy to do so.

There are special rules for the division of words in Bibles.

ERRATA, ERRATUM

NOTE that Errata, Addenda, and Corrigenda are plurals, and should only be used when listing a number of items; if there is only one, or when the list has been reduced to one by printing cancels, etc., the heading should be Erratum, Addendum, or Corrigendum.

There should be no point at the end of a line if the point forms no part of the correction; e.g. *for* at *read* near

But the point is sometimes the essential part of the correction, and then must be inserted; e.g. *for* Jones, *read* Jones.

FIGURES AND NUMERALS

WORDS OR FIGURES

Do not mix old-style and new-face figures in the same book without special[1] directions.

Nineteenth century, not 19th century.

Figures to be used when the matter consists of a sequence of stated quantities, particulars of age, etc.

---

[1] For example, when possible a different face *should* be used for superior figures indicating editions or manuscript sigla, to avoid confusion with footnote references. See also p. 145 (*n*).

Examples (for non-technical work):

Figures for September show the supply to have been 85,690 tons, a decrease in the month of 57 tons. The past 12 months show a net increase of 5 tons.

The smallest tenor suitable for ten bells is D flat, of 5 feet diameter and 42 cwt.

This applies generally to all units of measurement—tons, cwt., feet, as above, also of area, volume, time, force, electrical units, etc.

Separate objects, animals, ships, persons, etc., are not units of measurement unless they are treated statistically:

A four-cylinder engine of 48 b.h.p. compared with a six-cylinder engine of 65 b.h.p.

The peasant had only four cows.

A farm with 40 head of cattle.

Jellicoe's fleet consisted of twenty-four battleships against the German twenty-two, but six of the latter were pre-dreadnoughts. [Each battleship is identifiable individually; they are not simply units of measurement.]

But:

British losses were: sunk: 3 battle-cruisers, 3 cruisers, and 8 destroyers; and in casualties, killed and missing, 6,097; wounded, 510. [Here the losses of ships (although identifiable) seem to be rather units of measurement. The men killed and wounded, though individuals, are from the military point of view clearly casualties—units of measurement.]

In descriptive matter, numbers under 100 to be in words; but print '90 to 100', not 'ninety to 100'.

Spell out in such instances as:

With God a thousand years are but as one day.

I have said so a hundred times.

For fractions which are spelt out, print, e.g., three-quarters, two-thirds. When both a whole number and a fraction are spelt out, use a hyphen only in the fraction, e.g. one and three-quarters. Print combinations like half an inch, half a dozen, without hyphens.

NUMERALS GENERALLY

Insert commas with four or more figures, as 7,642 (but see pp. 58–9); print dates without commas, as 1908; omit commas in figures denoting pagination, column numbers and line numbers in poetry, and in mathematical workings, even though there may be more than three figures; also in library numbers, as: Harleian MS 24456.

Note a^8 (sheet) and a8 (leaf) in bibliographical matter.

Roman numerals to be preferred in such cases as Henry VIII—which should never be divided—and should not be followed by a full point unless the number ends a sentence. If, however, the author prefers the full title, use 'Henry the Eighth', not 'Henry the VIIIth'.

In decimals use the full point, as 7.06 (but see p. 87); and print 0.76, *not* .76. Similarly in printing the time of day: 4.30 p.m. and, with the 24-hour clock, 0.31, 22.15.

In degrees of temperature print 10.15 °C (not 10.15° C or 10°.15 C).

In dates, print: 25 June 1978.[1] Omit comma

---

[1] This will not apply to quotations, nor to reprints of documents. As to the form May 19, 1862, Sir James Murray said, 'This is not logical: 19 May 1862 is. *Begin* at day, *ascend* to month, *ascend* to year; not *begin* at month, *descend* to day, then *ascend* to year.'

between month and year: 'The delay after November 1967 was due to an oversight.'

In references to pagination, dates, etc., use the least number of figures possible; for example, print 30-1, 42-3, 132-6, 1841-5, 1960-1, 1966/7: but print, e.g., 10-11, *not* 10-1; 16-18, *not* 16-8; 116-18, *not* 116-8; 210-11, *not* 210-1; 314-15, *not* 314-5 (i.e. for the group 10-19 in each hundred). And do not contract dates involving different centuries, e.g. 1798-1810 *not* 1798-810. In displayed matter all dates should be in full: 1960-1961.

In collective numbers: *either* from 280 to 300, *or* 280-300; *not* from 280-300.

Print: 250 BC; but when it is necessary to insert AD the letters should precede the year, as AD 250.[1] Print a BC period with full figures, e.g. 185-122 BC; but a year of office thus: 117/16 BC, 49/8 BC (for use of *c.* (*circa*) with dates see p. 61).

When preliminary pages are referred to by lower-case roman numerals, no full points should be used after the numerals. Print: p. ii, pp. iii-x; *not* p. ii., pp. iii.-x.

When references are made to two successive text-pages print pp. 6, 7, if the subject is disconnected in the two pages; but if the subject is continuous from one page to the other then print pp. 6-7. In this the compositor must be guided by his copy. Print pp. 51 f. if the reference is to p. 51 and following page; but pp. 51 ff. when the reference is to more than a single page following.

In a sequence of figures use an en rule (-), as in the above examples; so also in such cases as Chapters III-VIII.

Begin numbered paragraphs: 1. 2. etc.; and clauses in paragraphs: (1) (2) (3), etc. If Greek or roman or italic lower-case letters are written, the compositor

---

[1] But print: first century AD.

must follow copy. Roman numerals (I, II, III) are usually reserved for chapters, important sections, and volumes.

References in the text to footnotes should be made by superior figures, which are to be placed outside the punctuation or quotation mark. Asterisks, superior letters, etc., may be used in special cases. The dagger and the other signs († ‡ § ¶ ||) should be used in mathematical works, to avoid confusion with the workings.

INDEXES[1]

EACH index is considered in relation to the book of which it is a part, and to the use required of it—which may vary from the simple Name and Place Index to the multiple special indexes of research publications and learned journals. Works on history and literature usually present a third category (viz. General Index) acting as a clearing-house of the information spread through perhaps many volumes of a wide-ranging work. The following recommendations are neither rigid instructions nor anything more than a starting-point for designing an individual index.

The index should begin on a right-hand page (but may begin on a left-hand page if necessary to make a fit or to avoid an oddment), and any subsequent indexes run on—if necessary on the same page (this again may depend on the fit of index to signatures). There is a tendency for specialized indexes to precede the general index.

The *heading* INDEX should be set in the same style as the book's preliminary titles.

---

[1] See BS 3700 The Preparation of Indexes to Books, Periodicals and Other Publications (1976), especially p. 7, on presentation and typography.

The *page number* is not to appear on the opening page (if not set on chapter-opening pages).

The left and right *headlines* throughout should be INDEX (or GENERAL INDEX, SUBJECT INDEX, INDEX OF PLACES, etc.).

The *number of columns* is usually two, but this can be varied to suit length of entries and width of page: only an index of first lines is normally set to the full measure. If there is adequate space between columns, there is no need to insert a rule.

Leaders (. . .) from items to page numbers are not used: page numbers are set close to their items.

Type: usually roman, at least one size smaller than text size, often the same as footnotes. Entries should be set solid by alphabetical sections (q.v.), with close word-spacing. Main references may be indicated by bold type and text-illustration numbers by italic, with roman capitals for plate numbers; but normally special type for keywords is not used. Phrases such as *see*, *see also*, etc., in italic.

Alphabetical sections: insert generally a line of white between sections. A displayed capital may be inserted if specifically asked for.

Entries (keywords, headwords) begin full left with lower case, unless proper names. Indent turn-over lines 1 em. (See *Sub-entries*.) The British Standard says: 'Punctuation is usually unnecessary between the last word or symbol of a heading or sub-heading and the page or other reference(s), but a comma may be used if confusion is likely without it, e.g. Vitamin B2, 76 (rather than Vitamin B2 76).'

Page reference figures should be separated by commas, *groups* of references by semicolons. A colon may be used to separate a keyword from explanatory matter, before the page references. Items in the run-on index (see *Repeated keywords*) are separated by semicolons. It is preferable to omit the full point at the end of a complete entry (except when this forms part of an abbreviation).

Sub-entries. There are two methods employed: (*a*) each sub-entry is run on after the keyword, keeping an indentation of 1 em throughout after the first line. Items are separated by semicolons. Thus sub-headings are not used. Advantages: simpler, space-saving. Disadvantage: time-consuming in use. (*b*), which is the more elaborate system, may use more space, but is quicker to consult. A keyword or keyphrase is terminated by a colon when there are no page references following, and is set full left (see *Entries, Page reference figures*). Each sub-entry should begin on a separate line, 1 em indented, with turnovers 2 ems. Further sub-sub-entries may begin on separate lines, 2 ems indented, with turnovers 3 ems (note that turnovers should be 3 ems throughout entries where sub-sub-entries occur). These deep indentations may be avoided by running on sub-sub-entries, separating items by semicolons, turnovers remaining at 2 ems.

Whichever is adopted, (*a*) or (*b*), sub-entries should be either in alphabetical order or in numerical order of the first page reference figure under each.

Mixture of two or more methods of dealing with sub-entries must be avoided.

Repeated keywords. The spaces of indentation imply repetition of keywords and sub-headings. This may also be indicated by em rules: these are set full out and repeated as required, with a thin space between. Each rule replaces the keyword or the sub-heading, as marked out by punctuation (see *Entries*).

Turnover. As a general rule the keyword(s), with the addition of '*(cont.)*:', should be repeated *only* at the top of the first column of a turnover (left-hand) page, set full left in a separate line. This rule will apply both to indexes with indented sub-entries and to indexes using em rules to indicate repetition of keywords (but see next paragraph). A '*(cont.)*' line will also be inserted where a left-hand page begins with a broken entry, even when it contains only a few lines. (In a *complicated* sequence of sub- and sub-sub-entries it may be helpful to repeat at the top of each column, but in this case special directions will be given.)

Where em rules are used to indicate the repetition of keywords, they should be retained at the heads of columns, with a '*(cont.)*' line inserted at the top of a left-hand column of a left-hand page (see above). The keyword, however, not a rule, will be placed at the top of the left-hand column of a left-hand page if the entry introduces a completely different person, or place, or subject with the same name, when it would be illogical to insert a '*(cont.)*' line.

ITALIC AND ROMAN TYPE

Use italic for:

Book-titles: *Pride and Prejudice*, *The Origin of Species*, or, Darwin's *Origin of Species*, *Robinson Crusoe* (the novel; but Robinson Crusoe the character in it).

Film and play titles: *Hamlet*, *Romeo and Juliet*.

Works of art: Picasso's *Guernica*, the *Discobolus*.

Long poems which are virtually books in themselves: *The Faerie Queene*, *Paradise Lost*, *The Lady of the Lake*, Dante's *Paradiso*, and any other poems divided into books or cantos.

Names of periodicals: apparent inconsistency is often caused by the prefix *The* being sometimes printed in italic and sometimes in roman. As a rule, print the definite article in roman lower case, as the *Daily Telegraph*, the *Daily Express*. *The Times* and *The Economist* are exceptions, as those publications prefer to have it so. *The*, if it is part of the title of a book, should also be in italic.[1] The title of an article appearing in a periodical should be in roman within quotation marks (but quotation marks may be omitted in bibliographies or lists of references).

Names of ships: in this case, print 'the' in roman, as it is often uncertain whether 'the' is part of the title or not. For example, the *King George V*, the *Revenge*; also put other prefixes in roman, as HMS *Dreadnought*. The possessive 's' to be also in roman, e.g. the *Majestic*'s crew. (See also p. 11.)

Stage directions in plays.

Words and short phrases in foreign languages (unless Anglicized): in particular this makes clear that a word is foreign when there is an English word spelt the same, e.g. the *Land* governments in West Germany (that is, those of the *Länder* which form the Federal Republic).

In mathematical works theorems are usually printed in italic.

For italic in biological nomenclature see p. 6; in musical works see p. 28.

Certain Latin words and their abbreviated forms: *ante, c. (circa), infra, passim, post, sic, supra, vide*. (Authors and editors should be encouraged to use rather the English forms for most of these: above, below, see, not *supra, infra, vide*. Sometimes, however, there is no exact equivalent, as for *passim*

---

[1] Henry Bradley and W. A. Craigie, joint editors of the *OED*, laid down the following rule: 'When the writer's intention is to quote the exact title as it stands, the article should be printed *The*; but when a work or periodical is merely referred to either as well known to the reader or as having been already mentioned, then the article should be left in roman (without initial capital, if not at the beginning of a sentence).'

and *sic*.) Italic *s*. and *d*. for shillings (*solidi*) and pence (*denarii*) come in this category (for decimal currency see p. 87).

Use roman in quotation marks for:

Titles of chapters in books, articles in periodicals, shorter poems (not long enough to be treated as book titles, see above), and short extracts from a text (italic being reserved for the title of the overall work): the 'Ode on the Intimations of Immortality' in *Lyrical Ballads*; D. E. Nineham's articles on 'Oral Tradition' in the *Journal of Theological Studies*; the famous chapter in *The Natural History of Ireland* entitled 'Concerning Snakes' which reads: 'There are no snakes to be met with throughout the whole island.'

Use roman (without quotation marks) for:

House names and public houses: The Firs, the Red Lion (see p. 45).

All the commonest short abbreviations: ad loc., app. crit., cf. (*confer*, compare), ed. cit., e.g., et seq., ibid., id., i.e., loc. cit., op. cit., q.v., sc., s.v., viz., unless otherwise directed.

FOREIGN WORDS AND PHRASES

The following to be printed in italic:

ab extra	*amour propre*	*bon ton*
ab initio	*ancien régime*	*brouhaha*
ab origine	*anglice*	*carte blanche*
ad hoc	*Angst*	*casus belli*
ad nauseam	*au courant*	*ceteris paribus*
ad valorem	*au fond*	*chef-d'œuvre*
affaire (de cœur)	*au revoir*	*chevaux de frise*
aficionado	*bête noire*	*chez*
a fortiori	*bêtise*	*con amore* (except
aide-mémoire	*bonhomie*	in music: see
amende honorable	*bon mot*	p. 29)

coup de grâce
coup de main
coup d'état
coup d'œil
crime passionnel
démarche
demi-monde
demi-pension
de quoi vivre
de rigueur
déshabillé
distrait(e)
dolce far niente
double entendre
echt
édition de luxe
élan
élan vital
en bloc
en fête
en masse
en passant
en rapport
en route
entente cordiale
esprit de corps
ex cathedra
ex officiis
ex parte[1]
facile princeps
factum est
fait accompli
felo de se
frisson
garçon
grand monde

habitué
hoi polloi
hors concours
hors de combat
idée fixe
idée reçue
imprimis
in propria persona
in situ
in vitro
in vivo
inter alia
jeu d'esprit
jeunesse dorée
joie de vivre
laissez-faire
laissez-passer
lapsus linguae
lèse-majesté
magnum opus
memento mori
métier
mise-en-page
mise-en-scène
modus operandi
modus vivendi
more suo
multum in parvo
naïveté
nemine
    contradicente
ne plus ultra
noblesse oblige
nolens volens
nom de plume
non est

nouveau riche
nouvelle vague
obiter dicta
objet d'art
outré
par excellence
pari passu
per contra
per se
piano nobile
pièce de résistance
pied-à-terre
pro tempore
raison d'être
rapprochement
rara avis
réchauffé
réclame
répétiteur
roman à clef
sans cérémonie
savoir-faire
sensu stricto
sine anno
sine die
sine qua non
sotto voce
sub rosa
tabula rasa
tour de force
tout court
trompe-l'œil
ultra vires
vis-à-vis
Weltanschauung
Zeitgeist

For further directions as to the use of italic for foreign words and phrases see pp. 24-5.

---

[1] Not italic for legal phrase: an ex-parte statement.

Print the following Anglicized words in roman:

aide-de-camp
al fresco (*one
   word attrib*.)
alias
apache
a posteriori
a priori
apropos
attaché
aurora borealis
avant-garde
beau idéal
bizarre
blasé
blitzkrieg
bloc
bona fide
bouillon
bourgeois
bourgeoisie
bric-à-brac
café
canard
cap-à-pie
carte-de-visite
chargé d'affaires
chatelaine
chiaroscuro
chic
claque
cliché
clientele
communiqué
concierge
confrère
consommé
contretemps
conversazione

cortège[1]
crèche
crêpe
cul-de-sac
curriculum
   vitae
débâcle
debris
début
débutant(e)
denouement
depot
detour
dilettante
doyen
dramatis
   personae
éclair
éclat
élite
ennui
ensemble
entourage
entrée
entrepôt
entrepreneur
ersatz
espresso
ex officio (*adv*.)
ex-officio (*adj*.)
exposé
extempore
fête
fiancé(e)
flair
fleur-de-lis
foyer
fracas

furore
gamin(e)
gendarme
genre
gratis
habeas corpus
hors-d'œuvre
imprimatur
in camera
incommunicado
kamikaze
lacuna
leitmotiv,
   -motif
levee
literati
literatus
littérateur
matinée
mêlée
ménage
milieu
mores
motif
naïve
née
nuance
obit (*noun*)
papier mâché
parvenu
passe-partout
pâté
patois
per annum
per capita
per caput
poste restante
post-mortem

[1] For a statement as to this and other French words now printed with a grave accent see p. 98.

pot-pourri
précis
prie-dieu
prima donna
prima facie
  (*adv.*)
prima-facie
  (*adj.*)
procès-verbal
pro forma
pro rata
protégé
quiche
raconteur

rapport
recherché
reconnaissance
regime
résumé
reveille
role
sang-froid
savant
seance
seriatim
soirée
soufflé
status quo

subpoena
terra firma
terrine
tête-à-tête
vade-mecum
verbatim
versus
via
vice versa
virtuoso
visa
viva voce
volte-face
wagon-lit

MUSICAL WORKS

USE initial capitals as follows: Beethoven's Ninth Symphony, Beethoven's Symphony No. 1 in C major, Beethoven's Op. 18 No. 1, Beethoven's Concerto for Violin and Orchestra; also for musical terms used as short titles of movements: Adagio, Allegro assai, Finale.

Use capitals for the names of keys, whether major or minor: E minor, not e minor.

The following should appear in italic:

  Titles of operas, ballets, song cycles, symphonic poems, oratorios, overtures.
  Abbreviated volume indications: *pp*, *mf*, etc. (these are always lower case).

The following should appear in roman, with single quotation marks:

  Titles of single songs.
  Popular names of works: e.g. the 'Jupiter' Symphony.
  Phrases denoting tempo marks (unless used as the name of a movement): 'allegro non troppo', 'più tranquillo'.

The following should appear in roman without quotation marks:

Musically descriptive titles: Piano Sonata Op. 111, Finale.

Technical terms and names of instruments: andante, cor anglais, forte, organum, shēng, vihuela.

Hyphens:

E flat, E major, etc., have no hyphens even when used adjectivally.

Folk-song (but folk music), ring-modulator.

Preferred spellings:

Delibes (no accent), George Frideric Handel, Orlandus Lassus, Josquin des Prez, Schoenberg, Skriabin, Stravinsky, Tchaikovsky, Vaughan Williams (no hyphen).

Aleatory, cantus firmus (plural cantus firmi), cello (no apostrophe), piano (not pianoforte), timpani, crotchet, twelve-note (not twelve-tone).

Plurals: Where the word is a commonly used term, form an English plural:

Appoggiaturas, intermezzos, sonatas, sopranos (see pp. 71–2).

NOR AND OR

'NEITHER' should be followed by 'nor', and 'either' by 'or':

Neither one thing nor the other.

I can neither read nor write.

Either Peter or James.

Note that when the alternatives form the singular

subject of a sentence the verb should be in the singular:

Neither Oxford nor Reading has been represented.

For further guidance see *Modern English Usage* (2/e, 1965) under each word.

O AND OH

USE O (*a*) when forming a vocative, and (*b*) when it is closely associated with and not separated by punctuation from what follows:

O mighty Caesar!
O God our help.
O worship the King!
O for the wings of a dove.

Use Oh as an independent exclamation, followed by a comma or exclamation mark:

Oh, snatch'd away in beauty's bloom.
Oh! how do you know that?

POETRY

WORDS ending in -ed are to be so spelt; a grave accent is sometimes used when the syllable is separately pronounced, thus: -èd.

This applies to poetical quotations in prose matter, and to new works. It must not apply to reprints of standard authors, nor to quotations in works which reproduce old spellings, etc. Neither must it apply to poems in which an author prefers his own method.

Whenever a poetic quotation is given a line (or more) to itself, it is not to be placed within quotation marks; but when the line of poetry runs on with the prose, or when a number of quotations follow one another and it is necessary to distinguish them, then quotation marks are to be used.

See also Appendix, pp. 152 ff.

POSSESSIVE CASE

U se 's for the possessive case in English names and surnames whenever possible; i.e. in all mono-syllables and disyllables, and in longer words accented on the penult as:

Charles's	Jones's
Cousins's	Thomas's
Gustavus's	St Thomas's
Hicks's	Thoms's
St James's Square	Zacharias's

In longer names not accented on the penult, 's is also preferable, though ' is here admissible; e.g. Nicholas'.

Euphony may decide the addition or omission of 's. It is often omitted when the last syllable of the name is pronounced -*iz*, as in Bridges', Moses'.

But poets in all these cases sometimes use s' only; and Jesus' is an accepted liturgical archaism. In quotations from Scripture follow the Oxford settings.

In ancient classical names use s' (not s's): Mars', Venus', Herodotus'. This is the prevailing custom in classical works.

Likewise ancient names in -es are usually written -es' in the possessive:

Ceres' rites	Xerxes' fleet

This form should certainly be used in words longer than two syllables:

Arbaces'	Miltiades'
Demosthenes'	Themistocles'

To pronounce another 's (= *iz*) after these is difficult.

French names ending in s or x should always be followed by 's when used possessively in English. Thus, it being taken for granted that the French pronunciation is known to the ordinary reader, and using Rabelais = Rabelè, Hanotaux = Anotō, Le Roux = Le Roo, Dumas = Dumah, as examples, the only correct way of writing these names in the possessive in English is Rabelais's (= Rabelèz), Hanotaux's (= Anotōz), Le Roux's (= Le Rooz), Dumas's (= Dumahz).

An apostrophe must not be used with the pronouns hers, ours, theirs, yours, its.

Apostrophes in place-names[1]

1. Use an apostrophe after the 's' in Queens' College (Cambridge). But:

2. Use an apostrophe before the 's' in: Connah's Quay (Clwyd), Hunter's Quay (Argyllshire), Land's End, Lord's Cricket Ground, Orme's Head (Gwynedd), The Queen's College (Oxford), St Abb's Head (Berwickshire), St John's (New-foundland), St John's Wood (London), St Michael's Mount (Cornwall), St Mungo's Well (Knaresborough).

3. Do not use an apostrophe in: All Souls (Oxford), Bury St Edmunds, Earls Court, Golders Green, Husbands Bosworth (Rugby), Johns Hopkins University (USA), Millers Dale (Derby), Owens College (Manchester), Palmers Green, St Albans, St Andrews, St Bees, St Boswells, St Helens (Merseyside), St Ives (Cambridgeshire and Cornwall), St Kitts (West Indies), St Leonards, St Neots (Cambridgeshire, but St Neot, Cornwall), Somers Town (London).

---

[1] The selection is arbitrary: but the examples are given on the authority of the Oxford University and Cambridge University Calendars, the *Post Office Guide*, *Crockford's Clerical Directory*, and the gazetteers in the Oxford Atlases. According to the Post Office, the old names for Scottish counties are still used.

PROOF CORRECTION

This section and some others (e.g. Scientific Work, pp. 54 ff.) are intended to be of assistance to authors, editors, and others who prepare manuscripts and handle proofs for the Press.

Corrections

USE ink or ball-point (avoid the use of pencil). A correction should be written in the nearer margin, the mark in the text merely indicating where the correction is to be made. If there is more than one correction in a line, marginal marks should appear from left to right in the same order.

The cost of corrections will be reduced if alterations can be so phrased as to fit the space left by deleted words.

Lengthy insertions are best typed on a separate sheet and attached to the proof (preferably by tape), their positions being clearly indicated in the text.

Draw a stroke (/) after each marginal mark to show that the correction is concluded. This is important where there are several corrections in a line.

Directions

Matter other than corrections (i.e. instructions to the printer or comments) should be preceded by the word 'PRINTER', and encircled. A different coloured ink is helpful for this purpose.

Queries

To accept a reader's query, strike out the question mark, leaving the correction that is to be made, thus:

To remove any possible doubt 'Yes' may be written against it.

PROOF-CORRECTION MARKS

(Where appropriate, the marks should also be used by copy-editors in marking up copy)

Instruction to Printer	Textual mark	Marginal mark
Correction made in error. Leave unchanged	- - - - under character(s) to remain	⊘
Remove extraneous marks or replace damaged character(s)	Encircle marks to be removed or character(s) to be changed	✗
(Wrong fount) Replace by character(s) of correct fount	Encircle character(s) to be changed	⊗
Insert in text the matter indicated in the margin	⋏	New matter followed by ⋏
Delete	Stroke through character(s) to be deleted	♂
Substitute character or substitute part of one or more word(s)	/ through character or ⊢——• through word(s)	New character or New word(s)
Set in or change to italic type	—— under character(s) to be set or changed	↲↲
Change italic to roman type	Encircle character(s) to be changed	≡≡
Set in or change to capital letter(s)	≡≡≡ under character(s) to be set or changed	╫
Change capital letter(s) to lower-case letter(s)	Encircle character(s) to be changed	≣
Set in or change to small capital letter(s)	≡≡ under character(s) to be set or changed	╪
Change small capital letter(s) to lower-case letter(s)	Encircle character(s) to be changed	∿
Set in or change to bold type	∿∿ under character(s) to be changed	∿∿
Set in or change to bold italic type	∿̄ under character(s) to be changed	∿∿∿

	Mark in text	Marginal mark
Invert type	Encircle character to be inverted	∩
Substitute or insert character in 'superior' position	/ through character or ⋋ where required	⅄ under character (e.g. -9̣)
Substitute or insert character in 'inferior' position	/ through character or ⋋ where required	L over character (e.g. -ĝ)
Insert full point or decimal point	⋋ where required	⊙
Insert colon, semi-colon, comma, etc.	⋋ where required	⊙ /;/ ·/ ‹/›/ [/]
Rearrange to make a new paragraph here	⌐ before first word of new paragraph	
Run on (no new paragraph)	ↄ between paragraphs	
Transpose characters or words	⌐ between characters or words to be transposed, numbered where necessary	
Insert hyphen	⋋ where required	|-|
Insert rule	⋋ where required	1 em, 4 mm (i.e. give the size of the rule in the marginal mark)
Insert oblique	⋋ where required	⊘
Insert space between characters		between characters	Y
Insert space between words	Y between words	⊢
Reduce space between characters		between characters	⊢
Reduce space between words	T between words	
Equalize space between characters or words		between characters or words	⋋

MARKS USED IN THE CORRECTION OF PROOFS

Adapted from JOHNSON's *Typographia* (1824),
Vol. II, p. 216

THOUGH a variety of opinions exist as to
the individual by whom the art of printing was
first discovered; yet all authorities concur
in admitting Peter Schoeffer to be the person
who invented *cast metal types*, having learned
the art of *cutting* the letters from the Guttembergs; he is also supposed to have been
the first who engraved on copper plates. The
following testimony is preserved in the family,
by Jo. Fred. Faustus of Ascheffenburg:
Peter Schoeffer of Gernsheim, perceiving
his master Fausts design, and being himself
desirous ardently to improve the art, found
out (by the good providence of God) the
method of cutting (*incidendi*) the characters
in a *matrix*, that the letters might easily be
singly *cast*, instead of being cut. He privately *cut matrices* for the whole alphabet:
Faust was so pleased with the contrivance
that he promised Peter to give him his only
daughter Christina in marriage, a promise
which he soon after performed.
But there were many difficulties at first
with these *letters*, as there had been before
with wooden ones; the metal being too soft
to support the force of the impression: but
this defect was soon remedied, by mixing
a substance with the metal which sufficiently
hardened it;

*and when he shewed his master
the letters cast from these matrices,*

THE OPPOSITE PAGE
CORRECTED

From JOHNSON'S *Typographia* (1824),
Vol. II, p. 217

THOUGH a variety of opinions exist as to the individual by whom the art of printing was first discovered; yet all authorities concur in admitting PETER SCHOEFFER to be the person who invented *cast metal types*, having learned the art of *cutting* the letters from the Guttembergs: he is also supposed to have been the first who engraved on copperplates. The following testimony is preserved in the family, by Jo. Fred. Faustus of Ascheffenburg:

'PETER SCHOEFFER of Gernsheim, perceiving his master Faust's design, and being himself ardently desirous to improve the art, found out (by the good providence of God) the method of cutting (*incidendi*) the characters in a *matrix*, that the letters might easily be singly *cast*, instead of being *cut*. He privately *cut matrices* for the whole alphabet: and when he showed his master the letters cast from these matrices, Faust was so pleased with the contrivance that he promised Peter to give him his only daughter *Christina* in marriage, a promise which he soon after performed. But there were as many difficulties at first with these letters, as there had been before with *wooden ones*; the metal being too soft to support the force of the impression: but this defect was soon remedied, by mixing the metal with a substance which sufficiently hardened it.'

To reject a reader's query, strike out the whole query; 'No' may be written against it, thus:

PUNCTUATION

Comma

GENERALLY, commas should be inserted between adjectives preceding and qualifying a substantive, as:

An enterprising, ambitious man.
A gentle, amiable, harmless creature.
A cold, damp, badly lighted room.

But where the last adjective is in closer relation to the substantive than the preceding ones, omit the comma, as:

A distinguished foreign author.
He was sorry for the little old lady.

Where *and* joins two single words or phrases the comma is usually omitted:

The honourable and learned member.

But where more than two words or phrases or groupings occur together in a sequence a comma should precede the *and* (the omission of the second comma in the second example would render the sentence ambiguous):

A great, wise, and beneficent measure.
New shops were opened by French and Collett, Booth and Tucker, and Jones.
The following sentence, containing two conjunctive *and*'s, needs no commas:

God is wise and righteous and faithful.

A comma should be used in such sentences as the following:

Truth ennobles man, and learning adorns him.

The Parliament is not dissolved, but only prorogued.

I believed, and therefore I spoke.

The question is, Can it be performed?

My son, give me thy heart.

The Armada being thus happily defeated, the nation resounded with shouts of joy.

Virtue is the highest proof of a superior understanding, and the only basis of greatness.

In some cases, however, two or more commas are necessary:

The French, having occupied Portugal, began to advance into Spain.

Be assured, then, that order, frugality, and economy are the necessary supporters of every personal and private virtue.

Such words as moreover, however, etc., are usually followed by a comma when used as the first word of a sentence, and preceded and followed by a comma when used later in a sentence. For instance:

In any case, however, the siphon may be filled.

When it means 'to whatever extent' however needs no following comma:

Bring the siphon, however full it is.

Commas are often used instead of parentheses:

Perhaps the most masterly, and certainly the easiest, presentation of the thought is in . . .

When a preposition is used as an adverb a comma should follow it, to avoid ambiguity:

In the valley below, the villages looked very small.

Omit the comma in such phrases as 'my friend Lord Oxford', 'my son John'.

Omit the comma when printing house numbers in addresses: 44 High Street.

Semicolon

The semicolon separates two or more clauses which are of more or less equal importance and are linked as a pair or series:

Truth ennobles man; learning adorns him.

Economy is no disgrace; for it is better to live on a little than to outlive a great deal.

The temperate man's pleasures are always durable, because they are regular; and all his life is calm and serene, because it is innocent.

Those faults which arise from the will are intolerable; for dull and insipid is every performance where inclination bears no part.

To err is human; to forgive, divine.

Never speak concerning what you are ignorant of; speak little of what you know; and whether you speak or say not a word, do it with judgement.

Semicolons divide the simple members of a compound sentence, and a dash may follow the last clause before the general conclusion:

To give an early preference to honour above gain, when they stand in competition; to despise every advantage which cannot be attained without dishonest arts; to brook no meanness, and stoop to no dissimulation—these are the indications of a great mind.

The sign ⸵ (*punctus elevatus*),[1] which occurs occa-

---

[1] The use of the *punctus elevatus* is described by P. Clemoes, *Liturgical Influence on Punctuation in Late Old English and Early Middle English Manuscripts* (Cambridge, 1952).

sionally in Old English manuscripts and frequently in Middle English manuscripts, is not a semicolon and should not be replaced by ;.

Colon

Whereas the semicolon links equal or balanced clauses, the colon generally marks a step forward, from introduction to main theme, from cause to effect, premiss to conclusion, etc., e.g.:

> In business there is something more than barter, exchange, price, payment: there is a sacred faith of man in man.

> Study to acquire a habit of thinking: no study is more important.

> It is regularly used to introduce examples, as:

> Always remember the ancient maxim: Know thyself.

A dash should not be added to a colon which is being used to introduce a list.

Full point[1]

Examples of its ordinary use:

> Fear God. Honour the King. Pray without ceasing.

> There are thoughts and images flashing across the mind in its highest moods, to which we give the name of inspiration. But whom do we honour with this title of the inspired poet?

Question mark

Examples of its ordinary use:

> Shall little, haughty ignorance pronounce
> His work unwise, of which the smallest part
> Exceeds the narrow vision of the mind?

[1] An abbreviation point preceding a quotation mark closes a sentence and an extra point outside the quote is unnecessary, e.g. . . . in 'titles of works, etc.' The sentence point is, however, required after a parenthesis, e.g. . . . titles (of works, etc.).

Was the prisoner alone when he was apprehended?
Is he known to the police? Has he any regular
occupation?

What does the pedant mean?

Cases where the note of interrogation must not be
used, the speaker simply stating a fact:

The Cyprians asked me why I wept.

I was asked if I would stop for dinner.

Exclamation mark

Examples of its ordinary use:

Hail, source of Being! universal Soul!

Alas for his poor family!

O excellent guardian of the sheep!—a wolf!

Alas, my noble boy! that thou shouldst die!

Ah me! she cried, and waved her lily hand.

O despiteful love! unconstant womankind!

Apostrophe[1]

Apostrophes in contractions similar to the following
should join close up to the letters: don't, 'em,
haven't, o'er, shan't, shouldn't, 'tis, won't, there'll,
I'd, I'll, we'll, I've, you've, he's, she's, it's, William's
(William is, has).[2]

Parentheses[3]

Examples:

I have seen charity (if charity it may be called)
insult with an air of pity.

Left now to himself (malice could not wish him
a worse adviser), he resolves on a desperate
project.

---

[1] See also Possessive Case, pp. 31 f.

[2] See also pp. 103, 105, 113, 117, 136.

[3] Printers call () parentheses, [] square brackets, and ⟨ ⟩ angle
brackets.

Occasionally parentheses occur within parentheses, as in the following: (*Wheaton* v. *Peters* (1834), 8 Peters, 591); (Copyright Act 1911, 6. 26 (2)). In the latter instance a hair space should divide the two parentheses falling together at the end.

Square brackets

These marks are used chiefly to enclose an explanation by someone other than the author. For example:

Perhaps (alarming thought!), perhaps he [Death] aims
Ev'n now the fatal blow that ends my life.
They [the Lilliputians] rose like one man.

Dash

The en-rule (-) is used (*a*) to denote a span, e.g. 'folios 23–94'; (*b*) to specify a period by connecting two terminal dates, e.g. 'the 1939–45 Holocaust'; (*c*) between separate places or areas linked, e.g., in a political context, 'the Rome–Berlin axis'; (*d*) between the names of joint authors to avoid confusion with the hyphen of a single double-barrelled name, e.g. 'the Temple–Hardcastle project' (that is, the project of Mr Temple and Mr Hardcastle).

Em rules or dashes—in this and the next line an example is given—are often used to show that words enclosed between them are to be read parenthetically. In the following example the dashes help to clarify a somewhat involved sentence:

Early in August M. Krestinski, the Soviet Ambassador in Berlin, who in consequence of the incident had been—not recalled but—granted leave of absence, returned to his post.

Thus the punctuation of a verbal parenthesis may be indicated in three ways: by em dashes, by (), or by commas.

Omit the dash when a colon is used to preface a quotation or similar matter, whether at the end of a break-line or not.

The dash is used chiefly to mark an interruption in the structure of a sentence.

Marks of omission

To mark omitted words three points . . . (not asterisks) separated by normal space of line are sufficient; and the practice should be uniform throughout the work. Where an initial is omitted as unknown two dots only should be used: such cases occur mainly in printing old documents. If a whole line of points is required to mark a large omission, real or imaginary, the spacing between the marks should be increased; but the compositor should still use full points, not asterisks.

When three points are used at the end of an incomplete sentence a fourth full point should not be added (unless the incomplete sentence is a quotation within an overall sentence, when the normal sentence point will be added after the final quotation mark); normal space of line should precede the first full point. But where the sentence is complete, the closing point is set close up, followed by three points for omission.

Quotation marks

Omit quotation marks for poetry, as instructed on pp. 30, 153. Also omit them for prose extracts broken off in smaller type, unless contrary instructions are given. When they are used, quotation marks should be repeated at the beginning of each new paragraph.

Insert quotation marks in titles of essays: e.g. 'Mr Brock read a paper on "Description in Poetry".' But omit quotation marks when the subject of the paper is an author: e.g. 'Professor Bradley read a paper on Jane Austen.' (See also p. 51.)

Quotation marks may be used to enclose slang and technical terms. They should not be used with house names or public houses: Chequers, Cosicot, the Barley Mow.

Single marks are to be used for a first quotation; then double for a quotation within a quotation. If there should be yet another quotation within the second quotation it is necessary to revert to single quotation marks.

Relative placing of quotation marks and punctuation

All signs of punctuation used with words in quotation marks must be placed *according to the sense*. If an extract ends with a point or exclamation or interrogation sign, let that point be included before the closing quotation mark; but not otherwise. When there is one quotation within another, and both end with the sentence, put the punctuation mark before the first of the closing quotation marks. These are important directions for the compositor to bear in mind; and he should examine the examples given in the pages that follow:

   'The passing crowd' is a phrase coined in the spirit of indifference. Yet, to a man of what Plato calls 'universal sympathies', and even to the plain, ordinary denizens of this world, what can be more interesting than those who constitute 'the passing crowd'?

   If the physician sees you eat anything that is not good for your body, to keep you from it he cries, 'It is poison!' If the divine sees you do anything that is hurtful for your soul, he cries, 'You are lost!'

   'Why does he use the word "poison"?'

   But I boldly cried out, 'Woe unto this city!'

   Alas, how few of them can say, 'I have striven to the very utmost'!

Thus, notes of exclamation and interrogation are sometimes included in and sometimes follow quotation marks, as in the sentences above, according to whether their application is merely to the words quoted or to the whole sentence of which they form a part. The sentence-stop must be omitted after ? or ! even when the ? or ! precedes the closing quotation marks.

In regard to other marks, when a comma, full point, colon, or semicolon is required at the end of a quotation, there is no reason for perpetuating the bad practice of their undiscriminating inclusion within the quotation marks at the end of an extract. So place full points, commas, etc., according to the examples that follow.

(i) Example: Our subject is the age of Latin literature known as 'Silver'. The single word 'Silver', being very far from a complete sentence, cannot have a closing point belonging to it: the point belongs to the whole sentence and should go outside the quotation marks: . . . known as 'Silver'.

(ii) If the quotation is intermediate between a single word and a complete sentence, or it is not clear whether it is a complete sentence or not, judgement must be used in placing the final point:

> We need not 'follow a multitude to do evil'.

The words quoted are the greater part of a sentence— '[Do not] follow a multitude to do evil'—but not complete in themselves, so do not require their own closing point; the point therefore belongs to the main sentence, and is outside the quotation marks.

Similarly in:

> No one should 'follow a multitude to do evil', as the Scripture says.
>
> Do not 'follow a multitude to do evil'; on the contrary do what is right.

Here the comma and semicolon do not belong to the quoted words and are outside the quotation marks.

(iii) The quoted words may be a complete sentence but the closing point must be omitted because the main sentence is not complete:

You say 'It cannot be done': I say it can.

Here the colon clearly belongs to the main sentence, forming the punctuation between 'You say' and 'I say', and is therefore outside the quotation marks.

(iv) When a quotation is broken off and resumed after such words as 'he said', if it would naturally have had any punctuation at the point where it is broken off, a comma is placed within the quotation marks to represent this.

Example: The words to be quoted are: 'It cannot be done; we must give up the task.' In quotation this might appear as:

'It cannot be done,' he said; 'we must give up the task.'

Note that the comma after 'done' belongs to the quotation, which has a natural pause at this point, but the semicolon has to be placed after 'said' and hence outside the quotation marks.

On the other hand, if the quotation is continuous, without punctuation at the point where it is broken, the comma should be outside the quotation marks.

Example: The words to be quoted are: 'Go home to your father.' In quotation these appear as:

'Go home', he said, 'to your father.'

The comma after 'home' does not belong to the quotation and therefore comes outside the quotation marks.

These rules, though somewhat lengthy to state in full, are simply instances of the maxim—*place punctuation according to sense.*

(v) The quoted words may be a complete sentence which ends at the same point as the main sentence:

He said curtly, 'It cannot be done.'

Logically, two full points would be required, one inside the quotes belonging to the quoted sentence, and one outside belonging to the main sentence. In such cases the point should be set *inside* the quotation marks (as ! or ? would be) and the point closing the main sentence omitted.

In particular, when a long sentence is quoted, introduced by quite a short phrase, it is better to attach the closing point to the long sentence:

Jesus said, 'Do not think that I have come to annul the Law and the Prophets; I have come to fulfil them.' (Not '. . . to fulfil them'.)

(vi) Where *more than one sentence* is quoted, the first and intermediate sentences will naturally have their closing points within the quotation, and the last sentence should do so also:

Moses told you: 'Do not kill. Do not steal. Do not commit adultery.' (Not '. . . adultery'.)

(vii) When a quotation is followed by a reference, giving its source, in parentheses, if it is a complete sentence, the closing quote is placed according to the above rules, before the parenthesis, and there is another closing point inside the parentheses:

'If the writer of these pages shall chance to meet with any that shall only study to cavil and pick a quarrel with him, he is prepared beforehand to take no notice of it.' (*Works of Charles and Mary Lamb*, Oxford edition, i. 193.)

(viii) Where marks of omission (or more rarely 'etc.') are used, they should be placed within the quotation marks if it is clear that the omitted matter forms part of the quotation.

Punctuation in classical and philological notes

In notes on English and foreign classics, as a rule[1] follow the punctuation in the following examples:

5. *Falls not*: lets not fall. (That is, a colon is usual after the lemma where a simple definition follows.)

17. *swoon*. The spelling of the folios is 'swound'. (Here a full point is used, because the words that follow the lemma constitute a complete sentence.)

Note that the initial letter of the word or phrase treated (as in *Falls not* and *swoon* above) should be in agreement with the text.

The lemma should be set in italic or bold type, according to directions.

Punctuation marks and references to footnotes
in juxtaposition

The relation of these to each other is dealt with on p. 20. Examples of the right practice are to be found on many pages of the present work.

Points in title-pages, headlines, etc.

All points (other than marks of interrogation or exclamation) are to be omitted from the ends of lines in titles, half-titles, page-headings, and cross-headings, unless a special direction is given to the contrary.

QUOTATIONS

QUOTATIONS in prose should not be broken off from the text unless the matter exceeds five lines. But short prose quotations (less than five lines) may be broken off if the context demands it, i.e. if the author sets them out, as it were, as examples

---

[1] There are alternative styles and an author may use one of them if he uses it consistently.

or specimens. Conversely, if the author weaves the quotations into his own paragraphs or even sentences, making it awkward to break them off, even longer extracts can be run on in the text in quotes.

When broken off, i.e. begun on a fresh line with the text on a fresh line following, quotations are distinguished, usually, by setting them in smaller type, full measure. Extracts treated in this way do not need to be enclosed by quotation marks (and therefore any quotations within them should be in single quotation marks, not double for quotes within quotes).

Any words of his own interpolated by the author in a quotation must be set in [] to show that they are not part of the quoted matter.

If two or more broken-off quotations follow without the author's own text intervening, and these are not continuous in the original, as there are no quotes to close and reopen the separation must be shown by leading.

If either of the last two paragraphs occasions difficulty, then the quoted matter must be set in (single) quotes in the normal way even though broken off.

The above rules apply to verse quotations with the addition that even a single line of poetry can be broken off, and if so, needs no quotes (but see Poetry, pp. 30, 153).

REFERENCES TO PRINTED AND MANUSCRIPT SOURCES[1]

Printed works

REFERENCES to books should normally be in the form Stubbs, *Constitutional History*, vol. ii, p. 98; or (if the context justifies it, i.e. the reader can be

[1] And see BS 1629 Bibliographical References (1976).

assumed to be familiar with the abbreviated title)
Stubbs, *Const. Hist.* ii. 98. (When any abbreviations,
other than the most common, such as *OED*, *DNB*,
are used for book titles, they should be listed and
explained.) Whichever style is adopted should be
uniform throughout the work, except that the system
may be used of giving the first reference in full, and
abbreviating thereafter.

In science books book-titles, whether appearing
in the body of the text, including footnotes, or in
bibliographies, 'further reading' lists, etc., will be
printed with capital initial letters for the first word
and proper names only. In all other classes of work
it will be the practice to capitalize the first and all
chief words.

The title of an article in a periodical should be
printed in roman within single quotation marks, with
the important words capitalized, and the title of the
periodical (whether abbreviated or not) in italic:
E. J. Dobson, 'A New Edition of "The Owl and
the Nightingale"', *Notes and Queries*, ccvi (1961),
444–8. In scientific works, titles of papers are printed
without quotation marks, and with capital initials
for proper nouns only.

Arabic figures in either bold or ordinary type are
used for volume numbers of scientific periodicals.

An author of a book to be published by the Press
is advised to adopt the system of references indicated
above.

Mention of the place of publication as well as the
publisher is frequently useful to the reader.

Examples (of printed works):

G. Cary, *The Medieval Alexander* (Cambridge,
1956), 54.

M. S. Serjeantson, 'The Dialects of the West
Midlands in Middle English', *RES* iii (1927),
331.

William Twiti, *L'Art de vénerie*, ed. G. Tilander (Uppsala, 1956).

Note that, as in these examples, p. for page may be omitted, especially when there is a volume number, ii. 98 being read as vol. ii, p. 98.

But in some standard works columns are numbered and ii. 98 would then refer to vol. ii, col. 98. This should cause no confusion as anyone turning up the reference will see the printed column numbers and not page numbers: beware, however, of inserting 'p.' in such cases. The author should be consulted if necessary.

Citation of authorities at the end of quotations should be printed in full, thus: HOMER, *Odyssey*, ii. 15. This chiefly applies to quotations at heads of chapters, but in references in notes print Hom. *Od.* ii. 15.

In poetry and plays, instead of volume and page, act and/or scene and line will be referred to, as follows:

References to Shakespeare's plays: *2 Henry VI*, III. ii. 14; and so with other references to act, scene, and line.

References to poems divided into books, cantos, and lines: Spenser, *Faerie Queene*, IV. xxvi. 35.

Without other directions references to the Bible in ordinary works should be printed thus: Job 32: 22; 37: 2, 17; 39: 38–9. (For full list of abbreviations see pp. 5–6.)

References to MSS or unprinted documents should be in roman.

The spacing of references is to be as follows:

4 n.; 5 f.; 6 sq.: thin space to precede n., f., sq.

4 n. 5; 5 et seq.; 12 and n. 7; p. 15 n. 3: ordinary space of line.

For use of italic see also pp. 23 ff.

In the citation of Acts of Parliament, note the use of arabic figures for chapter numbers in Public (General) and Private Acts (e.g. 3 & 4 Geo. V, c. 12, ss. 18, 19) and small roman numerals in Public (Local) Acts (e.g. 3 & 4 Geo. V, c. xii, ss. 18, 19). Scots Acts prior to the Union of 1707 are cited by year (*anno Domini*) and chapter, thus: 1532, c. 40.

In references to law reports care should be taken to distinguish between round and square brackets. In the Law Reports published by the Incorporated Council of Law Reporting from the year 1891 onwards, the date is a necessary part of the description of the volume. The date is placed within square brackets, and where there is more than one volume in a year, the number of the volume follows the date: e.g. *Rose* v. *Buckett* [1901] 2 KB 449. The same rule is followed by the Irish Council of Law Reporting from 1894 onwards: e.g. *R.* v. *Allen* [1921] 2 IR 241; and in one or two other series. In almost all other series (including those published by the Incorporated Council of Law Reporting before 1891) the volumes are serially numbered without the date being expressed; but as it is almost impossible to remember off-hand the date of a case cited merely by the volume, in recent books it has become a regular practice, and one to be strongly recommended, to add the date in round brackets after the name of the case: e.g. *Croft* v. *Dunphy* (1932) 102 LJPC 6. Thus the round brackets give real dates, the square often a false date, for cases are often reported in the volume of the year following their delivery.

Cases from the Scottish Series of Session Cases from the year 1907 onwards are cited as follows: *Hughes* v. *Stewart*, 1907 SC 791; Justiciary Cases, from 1917 onwards, as: *Corcoran* v. *HM Advocate*, 1932 JC 42. It is usual to refer to Justiciary Cases (i.e. criminal cases before the High Court of Justiciary) simply by the name of the panel (or accused), thus: *Corcoran*.

MS and unpublished sources

References to ancient MSS subsequently printed (as distinct from the printed editions thereof), old unpublished letters, etc., or modern ones deposited in libraries but not published, should not be set in italic. Examples:

Bodl. MS Rawlinson D. 520, fo. 7.

MS Bodley 34, fo. 14^{r-v}.

BL MS Cott. Vitellius A. xiv, fos. 123^v-125^r.

Lieut. Frewen's Diary, 3 June 1916 (unpublished; but *Diary* would imply that it was published).

Personal letter to the author, 28 Nov. 1964.

B. A. Smith, 'The Influence of the RC Church on Anglican Doctrine' (Univ. of Leeds MA thesis, 1936).

Government and official papers

In printing references to Command Papers, the author's use of C., Cd., Cmd., Cmnd., and Cm. must be followed. These distinctions are significant in that they each represent a different series.

SCIENTIFIC WORK

Copy should be clear. Special mathematical symbols and formulae may on occasion have to be written in by hand. Writing formulae by hand permits more flexibility, but the author should remember that the compositor is a layman, and has no context to guide him; hence the need for care in writing.

Many capital letters (C K M O P S U V W X Y Z) can easily be confused with lower case; and O, *o*, o, o (fig.); e, l, ɪ; x, X are easily confused unless their size and form are clearly indicated.

Symbols should be unmistakable. Care should be taken to distinguish between italic *a*, Greek *α*; italic *w*, Greek *ω*; and many other confusable characters.

Most mathematical symbols are printed in italic; most chemical symbols in roman. If both occur and there is a danger of confusion, it is helpful if they are so marked in the copy.

All mathematical symbols that are not to be printed in italic should be so marked. Since the same letter may be called for in various founts (e.g. bold face for vectors), the standard printer's markings should be used (wavy underline x for bold face **x**, etc.).

Two-line fractions in the text should be avoided to reduce work (and improve general appearance), e.g. the forms $\dfrac{a}{b}$, $\left|\dfrac{x-1}{3}\right|$, etc., should, by the use of the solidus, be replaced by a/b, $|(x-1)/3|$, etc. Simple fractions such as $\dfrac{\pi}{2}$, $\dfrac{x}{3}$, $\dfrac{a+b}{4}$, etc., are best printed as $\frac{1}{2}\pi$, $\frac{1}{3}x$, $\frac{1}{4}(a+b)$, etc.

Displayed formulae three or four lines deep can be reduced to the neater and much more manageable two-line form in almost all instances.

$$\frac{1-\tan^2\dfrac{A}{2}}{1+\tan^2\dfrac{A}{2}} \text{ should be written } \frac{1-\tan^2\frac{1}{2}A}{1+\tan^2\frac{1}{2}A};$$

$$\frac{\sin\dfrac{(N+1)}{2}\theta\,\sin\dfrac{N}{2}\theta}{\sin\dfrac{\theta}{2}}$$

should be written

$$\frac{\sin\frac{1}{2}(N+1)\theta\sin\frac{1}{2}N\theta}{\sin\frac{1}{2}\theta}.$$

Work can be reduced and appearance improved by writing such a formula as

$$\lim_{n\to\infty}\left\{1-\sin^2\frac{\alpha}{n}\right\}^{-\frac{1}{\sin^2\frac{\alpha}{n}}}$$

in the form

$$\lim_{n\to\infty}\{1-\sin^2(\alpha/n)\}^{-1/\sin^2(\alpha/n)}.$$

The rule (or vinculum) should be omitted from the square-root sign. Where necessary it may be replaced by parentheses:

e.g. $\sqrt{2}$ is sufficient for $\sqrt{2}$

and $\sqrt{\left(\dfrac{x^2}{a^2}+\dfrac{y^2}{b^2}\right)}$ for $\sqrt{\dfrac{x^2}{a^2}+\dfrac{y^2}{b^2}}$

and in each case the first form is more easily printed.

As far as possible any symbol which involves printing a separate line of type should be avoided when an alternative form is available:

e.g. for angle ABC $\angle ABC$ is preferable to $\widehat{ABC}$
or for vector r **r** (bold type) ,,   ,,   ,, $\vec{\mathrm{r}}$

The order of brackets in mathematical formulae is [{()}]. (For chemical formulae see below.) A single pair of brackets may have a specific meaning, e.g. [n] is used to denote the integral part of n.

Punctuation. A mathematical formula or equation, whether occurring in the text or displayed, should be regarded as in every way an integral part of the sentence in which it occurs, and be punctuated accordingly. Thus, individual formulae may be separated by commas, groups by semicolons, and where a formula occurs at the end of a sentence it should be followed by a full point.

In the case of displayed chemical formulae, how-ever, especially of the type

where the dots are part of the formula, punctuation marks may be, and frequently are, omitted.

In decimals the point should be set on the base line: 64.5.

Abbreviations of units. These should be consistent. They are printed in roman without a full point, and should remain unaltered in the plural:

5 cm (not 5 cm. nor 5 cms nor 5 cms.)

There are internationally agreed abbreviations for many units, including all those in the SI (the International System of Units). These include:

m	metre	t	tonne
g	gram	min	minute (of time)
s	second (of time)	h	hour
l	litre		

For a full list see the publications listed on p. 60. The prefixes used to form the names of multiples and submultiples of units are:

Multiple	*Prefix*	*Symbol*
× 10	deca	da
× 100 (10^2)	hecto	h
× 1000 (10^3)	kilo	k
× 10^6	mega	M
× 10^9	giga	G
× 10^{12}	tera	T
× 10^{15}	peta	P
× 10^{18}	exa	E

e.g.   kg = kilogram = 1000 grams
          MW = megawatt = 1 million watts
          GeV = giga-electronvolt = 1000 million
          electronvolts

$\div 10$ (i.e. $\times 10^{-1}$)	deci	d
$\div 100$ ($\times 10^{-2}$)	centi	c
$\div 1000$ ($\times 10^{-3}$)	milli	m
$\times 10^{-6}$	micro	μ
$\times 10^{-9}$	nano	n
$\times 10^{-12}$	pico	p
$\times 10^{-15}$	femto	f
$\times 10^{-18}$	atto	a

e.g.   mg = milligram = 1 thousandth of a gram
          μm = micrometre = 1 millionth of a metre
          pF = picofarad = 1 millionth of a micro-
          farad

(The micrometre or micron, 10^{-6} m, should not be represented by the symbol μ alone.)

Powers of units may be represented thus:

    m^2 square metre   cm^3 cubic centimetre

But in many contexts cc for cubic centimetre is permissible; and in less technical works sq yd may be preferable to yd^2.

A product of two or more different units may be represented thus:

    N m or N·m (not Nm) (newton-metre)

A quotient may be represented thus:

m/s or m·s^{-1} or m s^{-1} (not ms^{-1}) (metre per second)

No more than one solidus should be used in the same expression; parentheses are used to avoid ambiguity:

    J K^{-1} mol^{-1} or J/(K mol) but not J/K/mol

In printing numbers up to 9999 the figures should be set close up without a comma. In numbers above this, thin spaces should be used instead of commas: 1 000 000. (See also p. 18.)

Chemical formulae. Symbols for the elements are given in *ODWE* (see p. 139). In formulae they are printed in roman without spaces; e.g. H_2SO_4; $Cu(CrO_2)_2$. In certain kinds of name they are printed in italic; e.g. *O*-methylhydroxylamine. Italic is also used for certain prefixes, of which the commonest are

> *o*- (or *ortho*-)   *cis*-
> *m*- (or *meta*-)   *trans*-
> *p*- (or *para*-)

For example, *p*-diethylbenzene; *cis*-but-2-ene. The italic, but not the hyphen, is retained if the prefix is used as a separate word:

> the *cis* isomer
> position *a* is *ortho* to the methyl group

The order of brackets in formulae is normally {[()]}, but there are special rules regarding the use of square brackets in the formulae of co-ordination compounds.

Dots in formulae representing single bonds should be raised, not on the line, but they can often be dispensed with altogether:

$$R \cdot CH_2 \cdot COOCH_3 \quad \text{or} \quad RCH_2COOCH_3$$

Dots in the formulae of addition compounds cannot be dispensed with; e.g. $Na_2CO_3 \cdot 10H_2O$.

The mass number of an element, if shown with its symbol, should be printed as a left superscript; e.g. ^{235}U. If given with the name of the element, no hyphen is necessary; e.g. uranium 235. Ionic charge is shown by a right superscript; e.g. SO_4^{2-}.

In names like the following there should be no space before the first parenthesis:

> iron(II)   chloride
> iron(2 +) chloride

For more comprehensive recommendations see the following:

BS 1991 Letter Symbols, Signs and Abbreviations (1961–)

BS 3763 The International System of Units (1976)

BS 5775 Specification for Quantities, Units, and Symbols (1979–)

Quantities, Units, and Symbols, 2nd edn. (Royal Society, London, 1975)

Nomenclature of Organic Chemistry (IUPAC, Oxford, 1979)

Nomenclature of Inorganic Chemistry, 2nd edn. (IUPAC, London, 1971)

R. S. Cahn, *An Introduction to Chemical Nomenclature*, 4th edn. (London, 1974)

Handbook for Chemical Society Authors, Special Publication No. 14 (The Chemical Society, London, 1960)

SPACING[1]

WORD-SPACING must be even. Paragraphs are not to be widely spaced for the sake of making break-lines. Break-line spaces should normally be thick. In general, close spacing is to be preferred, with the space of the line after a full point; but this must be regulated according to the class of work.

Break-lines should consist of more than five letters, except in narrow measures.

Poetry should not be more than thick spaced.

If possible, avoid (especially in full measures) printing at the ends of lines: a, l., ll., p., *or* pp.

---

[1] See note on p. xi for explanation of terms used throughout this book.

Do not divide initials: W. E. | Gladstone *not*
W. | E. Gladstone.

Abbreviations of titles, such as MP, DD, MA, or
of occupations or parties, such as ICS, ILP, to have
no space between the letters.

When titles of books or journals are represented by
initials no space is to be put between the letters; e.g.
SBE, *JTS* (and *Cal. SP Dom.*).

When *c.* (*circa*) is used before numerals, it should
be printed close up to the numerals:

c.1600; 1600–c.1800; c.4 hr.; but *c.* Jan. 1986.

No spaces to be placed between lower-case abbreviations, as in e.g., i.e., q.v.

Indentation of first lines of paragraphs to be generally 1 em for full measures, with sub-indentation
proportionate. The rule for all indentation is not to
drive too far in.

SPECIAL SIGNS AND SYMBOLS

THE signs + (plus), − (minus), = (equal to),
> ('larger than', in etymology signifying 'gives' or
'has given'), < ('smaller than', in etymology signify-
ing 'derived from') are often used in printing biological and philological works, and not only in those
which are scientific or arithmetical.

In such instances +, −, =, >, < should not be
printed close up. For instance, in

spectabilis, *Bœrl. l.c.* (= Haasia spectabilis)

the = belongs to 'spectabilis' as much as to 'Haasia',
and the sign should not be put close to 'Haasia'.
A thin space only should be used.

In philological works an asterisk * prefixed to a
word signifies a reconstructed form; a dagger †
signifies an obsolete word. The latter sign, placed
before a person's name, signifies deceased.

In early medical books the formulae were set in lower-case letters, j being used for i both singly and in the final letter, e.g. gr. j (one grain), ʒviij (eight ounces), ʒiij (three drachms), ϑiij (three scruples), ℳiiij (four minims).

THORN, ETH, WYN, YOGH

IN the printing of Old English follow copy for the use of thorn (þ, capital Þ) and eth (ð, capital Ð). The combination *th* is rare in Old English and should be avoided unless specified by the author (e.g. in 'diplomatic' texts).

Except in special circumstances—e.g. in the few early Middle English works in which both *w* and wyn are used—*w* is normally to be substituted for the wyn (ƿ) of the manuscript. Similarly, in Old English works print *g*, not ȝ, except in the few works in which both letter-shapes occur.

In some early Middle English texts ȝ is permissible, but normally ȝ is to be used for yogh in all Middle English work.

VOWEL-LIGATURES[1] (Æ AND Œ)

THE combinations *æ* and *œ* should each be printed as two letters in Latin and Greek words, e.g. Aeneid, Aeschylus, Caesar, Oedipus, Phoenicia; and in English, as formulae, phoenix. Print, e.g., oestrogen

---

[1] The separately written *oe*, *ae* are 'digraphs', because the sounds they represent are in modern pronunciation *not* diphthongs, though they were such in classical Latin; but *ch*, *ph*, *sh* are also digraphs. Æ, æ, Œ, œ, are rather single letters than digraphs, though they might be called ligatured digraphs.

(where *oe* represents a single sound), but, e.g., chloro-ethane (not chloroethane) to avoid confusion.

In Old English words use the ligature *Æ*, *æ*, as Ælfric, Cædmon; and in French words use the ligature *œ*, as *œuvre*.

SPELLINGS

ALTERNATIVE AND DIFFICULT SPELLINGS

abetter
abettor (*in law*)
accepter (-or *in law and science*)
accessory (*not -ary in current use*)
accommodation
adapter (-or *electr.*)
adviser
ageing
agitator
align, -ment
alleluia
almanac (*but -ack for Oxford and Whitaker's*)
ambidextrous
ambience (-ance *as term in art*)
ampere (*unit*)
annex, *v.*
annexe, *n.*

apostasy
archaeology
arcing[1]
artefact
aught (*anything*)
ay (*yes*; pl. *the ayes have it*)
aye (*always*)
balk, *v.*
baulk (*timber*)
biased
bivouac, *n.*
bivouac (-cked), *v.*
bluish
bogey (*golf term*)
bogie (*wheeled undercarriage*), *pl.* -ies
bogy (*apparition*), *pl.* -ies
brier
calendar, *n. and v.* (*register*)
calender, *n. and v.* (*press*)
canvas, *n.* (*cloth*)

canvas, *v.* (*to cover with canvas*; *past* canvased)
canvass, *n. and v.* (*solicit(ing) votes*; *past* canvassed)
carcass (-es)
censer (*vessel*)
censor (*official*)
centigram
centred, centring
chameleon
cheque (*bank*)
chequered (*career*)
colander (*strainer*)
commitment
comparative
computer
conjuror
connection
conscientious
consensus
conterminous

---

[1] The normal formation would be *arcking* (to preserve the hard sound), but the *OED Supplement* (1972) prefers *arcing* and gives good evidence for this form.

convection
convector
convener
copier
cornelian
corslet
crosier
curb (*to restrain*)
curtsy
deflexion
dependant, *n.*
dependent, *a.*
depositary
 (*person*)
depository
 (*place*)
descendant
desiccate
dextrously
dike
dispatch
dissect
divest (*devest
 in law*)
draft (*prepare*)
draftsman (*one
 who drafts
 documents*)
draught (*of air;
 a drink*)
draughtsman
 (*one who draws
 plans, etc.*)
drier (*machine
 for drying*)
duffel
duress
dyeing (*cloth*)
ecology
ecstasy
educationist
embarrass

embed
enclose (*but
 inclosure of
 land*)
encroach
encrust (*but
 incrustation*)
encyclopaedia
endorse
enquire (*ask*)
enquiry
 (*question*)
enrol
ensure (*to make
 sure*)
envelop, *v.*
envelope, *n.*
erector
faecal, faeces
feldspar
fetid
fillip
flyer
foetal
foetus
fogy, *pl.* -ies
forbade
forbear, *v.* (*to
 abstain*)
forebear
 (*ancestor*)
forego (*to go
 before*)
foregone
 (*conclusion*)
forestall
foretell
forgather
forgo (*to go
 without*)
forme (*printer's*)
fount (*type*)

Francophile
fulfil
fullness
fungous, *a.*
fungus, *n.*
further
fusilier
fusillade
gaol
gaoler
genuflexion
gibe
gluing
glycerine
gram
gramophone
Gram's stain
grandad
grandam
granddaughter
granter (*one
 who grants*)
grantor (*in law*)
grey
grisly (*terrible*)
grizzly (bear;
 grey)
guerrilla
guild, *n.*
gypsy
haematite
haematology
haemorrhage
haemorrhoids
hallo
harass
hearken
hiccup
Hindu
honorific
horsy
humous, *a.*

humus, *n.*
idiosyncrasy
impinging
impostor
independent, *n.*
    and a.
inflexion
inquire (*investi-
    gate*)
inquiry (*formal
    investigation*)
install
instalment
instil
insure (*to take
    insurance*)
inure
investor
jalopy
jam, *v.* (*to block*)
jamb (*of door*)
Jew's harp
judgement
    (judgment *in
    legal works*)
jugful
kerb (*pavement*)
kilogram
kilometre
koala
Koran
lachrymose
lackey
lacquer
largess
latish
leger line (*mus.*)
licence, *n.*
license, *v.*
licensee

lich-gate
Linnaean (*but
    Linnean
    Society*)
liquefy
liquorice
loadstone
loath, *a.*
loathe, *v.*
lodestar
mackintosh
maharaja
mamma
mandolin
manikin (*little
    man*)
mannequin
    (*model*)
marijuana
marquis
matt, *a.*
medieval
millepede
milligram
mizen-mast
moneyed
moneys
mongoose(s)
mortgagee
    (*creditor in a
    mortgage*)
mortgager (-or *in
    law*; *debtor in
    a mortgage*)
mucous, *a.*
mucus, *n.*
Muhammad
Muslim
Mycenaean
naught (*nothing*)

nerve-racking
net (*profits*)
neurone
nought (*zero*)
noviciate
olefin
omelette
ouzel
oyez!
paediatric
palaeography
palaeology
paraffin
parakeet
partisan
pasha
pastille
pederast
peewit
pendant, *n.*
pendent, *a.*
peony
picnicking
postilion
pott (*size of
    paper*)
practice, *n.*
practise, *v.*
premises (*pl.
    only*)
premiss, -es
    (*logic*)
primeval
principal (*chief*)
principle (*basis
    of behaviour*)
printer's error,
    pl. printer's
    or printers'
    errors[1]

[1] Where there is any ambiguity a hyphen may be used: bad printers'-errors.

Privy Council
Privy Counsellor
programme
    (*but* program
    in computing)
proletariat
propellant, *n.*
propellent, *a.*
prophecy, *n.*
prophesy, *v.*
Punjab
putrefy
pygmy
pyjamas
questionnaire
queuing
racket (*bat*)
rackets (*game*)
radical
    (*chemistry*)
radicle (*botany*)
raja
rarefaction
rarefy
raze, *v.* (*in all
    senses; not
    rase*)
recompense
reflection
rhyme (*verse*)
rigor (*med.*)
rigour

rime (*hoar-frost*)
Romania
Romanian
routeing (*from
    route, v.*)
salvage (*of ships*)
savannah
scallop
selvage (*of cloth*)
sergeant
    (*military*)
serjeant (*law*)
settler (*one who
    settles*)
settlor (*in law*)
Shakespeare,
    -rian
show, *v.* and *n.*
sibyl
sibylline
silvan
silviculture
singeing
Sinhalese
skiing (*and* ski'd)
speleology
stanch (*to stop
    flow*)
stationary (*at
    rest*)
stationery (*paper*)
staunch (*true*)

steadfast
storey (*of
    house*)
strait-laced
superintendent
swingeing (*blow*)
sycamore
taxiing
timpani (*drums*)
tingeing
tranship(ment)
transonic
transsexual
transubstantiate
tsar
tympana (*pl. of
    tympanum*)
tyre
underlie (*but
    underlying*)
veld
vendor
veranda
vermilion
visor
wagon
whiskey (Irish
    and US)
whisky (Scotch)
whitish
wistaria
wooed, woos

DOUBLING OF CONSONANTS
WITH SUFFIXES

Words of one syllable

THOSE ending with one consonant preceded by
one vowel (not counting *u* in *qu*) double that

consonant on adding *-ed* or *-ing* unless it is *h, w, x,* or *y*:[1]

beg	begged	begging
clap	clapped	clapping
fit	fitted	fitting
squat	squatted	squatting
stop	stopped	stopping

but

stay	stayed	staying
stew	stewed	stewing
tow	towed	towing
toy	toyed	toying
vex	vexed	vexing
		(oohing and) ahing

This rule also applies to the suffixes *-er* and *-est*:

fat	fatter	fattest
fit	fitter	fittest
glad	gladder	gladdest

Monosyllabic words not ending with one consonant preceded by one vowel generally do not double the final consonant (e.g. clamp, clamped, clamping; squeal, squealed, squealing).

Words of more than one syllable

Those that end with one consonant preceded by one vowel double the consonant on adding *-ed*, *-ing*, or *-er* if the last syllable is stressed (but not if the consonant is *w, x,* or *y*):

allot	allotted	allotting
commit	committed	committing
infer	inferred	inferring
occur	occurred	occurring
omit	omitted	omitting
prefer	preferred	preferring
trepan	trepanned	trepanning

[1] But note bused, busing (in the sense 'transported, transporting, by bus').

but

array	arrayed	arraying
destroy	destroyed	destroying
guffaw	guffawed	guffawing
relax	relaxed	relaxing

But words of this class *not* stressed on the last syllable *do not double the last consonant*[1] on adding *-ed*, *-ing*, *-er*, or *-y* unless the consonant is *l*:

balloted, -ing	docketed, -ing	picketed, -ing
banqueted, -ing	faceted, -ing	pivoted, -ing
bayoneted, -ing	ferreted, -ing	proffered, -ing
benefited, -ing	fidgeted, -ing, -y	profited, -ing
biased, -ing	filleted, -ing	rabbeted, -ing
bigoted	filliped, -ing	rabbiting
billeted, -ing	focused, -ing	rickety
blanketed, -ing	galloped, -ing	ricocheted, -ing
bonneted, -ing	gibbeted, -ing	riveted, -ing
bracketed, -ing	gossiped, -ing, -y	russeted, -ing,
budgeted, -ing	helmeted	-y
buffeted, -ing	hiccuped, -ing	scalloped, -ing
carpeted, -ing	jacketed, -ing	thickened, -ing,
chirruped, -ing	junketed, -ing	-er
combated, -ing	lettered, -ing	trousered, -ing
cricketing, -er	marketed, -ing	trumpeted, -ing
crotcheted,	offered, -ing	visited, -ing
-ing, -y	packeted, -ing	wainscoted,
discomfited, -ing	paralleled, -ing[2]	-ing

In words ending in *-l* the last consonant is generally doubled whether stressed on the last syllable or not:

annulled, -ing	chiselled, -ing,	dishevelled, -ing
appalled, -ing	-er	empanelled, -ing
apparelled, -ing	compelled, -ing	enrolled, -ing
bevelled, -ing	counselled, -ing	extolled, -ing
channelled, -ing	cudgelled, -ing	fulfilled, -ing

[1] Exceptions are in- and outputting; worshipped, -ing, -er; and words ending with *l*.

[2] This is an exception to the rule relating to the doubling of *l*.

grovelled, -ing	libelled, -ing	revelled, -ing
impelled, -ing	marshalled, -ing	rivalled, -ing
initialled, -ing	modelled, -ing,	shovelled, -ing
instilled, -ing	-er	trammelled,
kennelled, -ing	panelled, -ing	-ing
labelled, -ing	parcelled, -ing	travelled, -ing,
levelled, -ing	quarrelled, -ing	tunnelled, -ing

Exceptions: appealed, -ing; paralleled, -ing; travailed, -ing.

FIFTEENTH- TO SEVENTEENTH-CENTURY WORKS

WHEN it is necessary to reproduce the spellings and printed forms of early writers the following rules should be observed:

Initial *u* is printed *v*, as in vnderstande. Also in such combinations as wherevpon.

Medial *v* is printed *u*, as in haue, euer.[1]

Initial and medial *j* are printed *i*, as in iealousie, iniurie, but in roman numerals *j* may be used finally, as viij.

In capitals the U is non-existent, and should always be printed with a V, initially and medially, as VNIVERSITY.

In ye and yt the second letter should be a superior, and without a full point.

FORMATION OF PLURALS IN ENGLISH

WORDS ENDING IN -E AND -Y

PLURALS of nouns ending in *-e* are formed by adding *-s*: divergence, divergences; excellence, excellences.

---

[1] Old manuscripts, however, are often inconsistent in the use of *u* and *v*, and where exact reproduction is needed the copy must be followed.

Nouns ending in -*y* preceded by a consonant form their plurals by changing *y* into *ies*: his Excellency, their Excellencies; ruby, rubies; story, stories. An exception is found in fly (a carriage), *pl.* flys. Proper names also retain *y*: the Carys, the Merrys, the three Marys.

WORDS ENDING IN -O

The plurals of nouns ending in -*o* are often confusing, owing to the absence of any settled system. The following is a list of common words with this ending, showing preferred spellings. Guidance on words not listed is given in the article -*o(e)s* in *Modern English Usage*, and the *Oxford Dictionary for Writers and Editors* gives the plurals of individual words ending in -*o*. (See also p. 29 for musical terms.)

albinos	crescendos	ghettos
altos	curios	goes
archipelagos	dados	gringos
armadillos	dagos	grottoes
arpeggios	dingoes	haloes
banjos	dodos	heroes
bastinados	dominoes	impresarios
boleros	duodecimos	innuendoes
bravoes (*hired*)	dynamos	kilos
bravos (*of the crowd*)	echoes	lassos
	egos	librettos[2]
buffaloes	electros	Lotharios
calicoes	embargoes	magnetos
cameos	embryos	mangoes
cantos	Eskimos	manifestos
cargoes	fiascos	medicos
centos	flamingos	mementoes
commandos	folios	memos
concertos[1]	frescos	mosquitoes

---

[1] But see p. 73 n. 5.

[2] This word can also take the plural libretti in some contexts.

mottoes
Negroes
noes
octavos
oratorios
peccadilloes
photos
pianos
piccolos
placebos
porticoes
potatoes

pros
provisos
punctilios
quartos
radios
ratios
Romeos
salvoes
  (*discharges*)
salvos (*reserva-
  tions, excuses*)
scenarios

solos[1]
sopranos[1]
stilettos
stuccoes
tiros
tomatoes
tornadoes
torpedoes
torsos
vetoes
volcanoes
zeros

COMPOUNDS

Compound words formed by a noun and an adjective, or by two nouns connected by a preposition,
form their plurals by a change in the chief word; e.g.
adjutants-general, aides-de-camp, courts martial,
cousins-german, fleurs-de-lis, men-of-war, poets-
laureate, sons-in-law.

Note that the singular form is used with a plural
number in such combinations as: an eight-foot stone,
a seven-inch gun, a six-mile track, a twelve-pound
shot.

FORMATION OF PLURALS IN
WORDS OF FOREIGN ORIGIN

PLURALS of nouns taken into English from other
languages sometimes follow the laws of inflexion of
those languages. But often, in non-technical works,
additional forms are used, constructed after the
English manner. Print as follows unless instructed
otherwise.

---

[1] These words can also take the plurals soli and soprani in some
contexts.

Singular	Plural
addendum	addenda[1]
——	agenda[2]
alga	algae
alkali	alkalis
alumnus	alumni
amanuensis	amanuenses
analysis	analyses
animalculum	animalcula
antithesis	antitheses
apex	apexes
aphis	aphides[3]
apparatus	apparatuses
appendix	appendices
arcanum	arcana
atrium	atria *or* atriums
automaton	automatons[4]
axis	axes
bacillus	bacilli
bandit	bandits
basis	bases
beau	beaux
broccoli	broccoli
bronchus	bronchi
bureau	bureaux
cactus	cacti
calculus	calculi
calix	calices
chateau	chateaux
chrysalis	chrysalides
coagulum	coagula
concerto	concertos[5]
corrigendum	corrigenda[1]
cortex	cortices
crematorium	crematoria

---

[1] See reference to these words on p. 16.

[2] Now commonly used as a singular noun meaning 'list of items for consideration'; in this sense *pl.* agendas is permissible.

[3] Of unknown etymology; aphid, *pl.* aphids, is also common.

[4] But automata when used collectively.

[5] But concerti grossi for plural of concerto grosso.

Singular	Plural
crisis	crises
criterion	criteria
crocus	crocuses
crux	cruces
curriculum	curricula
datum	data
desideratum	desiderata
dilettante	dilettantes *or* dilettanti
effluvium	effluvia
elenchus	elenchi
ellipsis	ellipses
encomium	encomiums
ephemera	ephemeras
ephemeris	ephemerides
epithalamium	epithalamia
equinox	equinoxes
erratum	errata[1]
focus	focuses[2] (*familiar*)
formula	formulas[2]
fungus	fungi
genius (*person*)	geniuses[3] (*persons*)
genus	genera
gladiolus	gladioli
gymnasium	gymnasiums
helix	helices
hiatus	hiatuses
hypothesis	hypotheses
ignis fatuus	ignes fatui
ignoramus	ignoramuses
imago	imagines (*entomology*), imagos (*psychology*)
index	indexes[2]
iris	irises
lacuna	lacunas *or* lacunae
lamina	laminae
larva	larvae

[1] See reference to this word on p. 16.

[2] But some words should retain their Latin plurals in their scientific sense: foci, formulae, indices, media, vortices.

[3] Genie, in the sense of a tutelary spirit or goblin, must have the plural genii.

Singular	Plural
lemma	lemmas[1]
maestro	maestri
matrix	matrices
mausoleum	mausoleums
maximum	maxima
medium	mediums[2] (*familiar*)
memorandum	memorandums[3]
metamorphosis	metamorphoses
miasma	miasmata
minimum	minima
narcissus	narcissi
nebula	nebulae
nucleus	nuclei
oasis	oases
octopus	octopuses
papilla	papillae
parenthesis	parentheses
parhelion	parhelia
phenomenon	phenomena
plateau	plateaux
radius	radii
radix	radices
ranunculus	ranunculuses[4]
referendum	referendums
sanatorium	sanatoriums
scholium	scholia
series	series
spectrum	spectra
speculum	specula
stamen	stamens
stimulus	stimuli
stratum	strata
syllabus	syllabuses
synopsis	synopses
tableau	tableaux

[1] But lemmata in lexicography.

[2] See p. 74 n. 2. Media is the collective plural in the sense 'channels of information'.

[3] Meaning separate notes, but in a collective or special sense print memoranda.

[4] But print ranunculi if consistently so in the copy.

Singular	*Plural*
terminus	termini
thesis	theses
ultimatum	ultimatums
virtuoso	virtuosi
virus	viruses
vortex	vortexes[1] (*familiar*)

HYPHENED AND NON-HYPHENED WORDS

(i) The hyphen is used in compounds used attributively, to clarify the unification of the sense. Thus an adverb qualifying an adjective does not normally need to be joined to it with a hyphen if the sense is already clear, as in 'a beautifully furnished house'. But where the adverb might not at once be recognized as such, and forms a single concept with the adjective, a hyphen is necessary, e.g. a well-known statesman, an ill-educated fellow, a new-found country.

(ii) Where an adverb qualifies a predicate, the hyphen should not be used, as in 'this fact is well known'. Use of the hyphen varies in other compounds according to whether they are used attributively or predicatively.

Compare:

> These are the most up-to-date records (*attrib.*).
> The records are not up to date (*predic.*).

(iii) Where a noun and an adjective (or a participle), or an adjective and a noun are used attributively in combination, the hyphen should be used, e.g. a poverty-stricken family, a blood-red hand, a large-scale map. This rule applies also to adjectival combinations of colours used attributively, e.g.

---

[1] See p. 74 n. 2.

bluish-grey haze (but: the haze was bluish grey). Another adjective or an adverb preceding the combination is not usually hyphenated with it, e.g. a late nineteenth-century invention (an exception is mid, which is joined with a hyphen, as in 'a mid-fifteenth-century church'). For the use of hyphens in fractions see p. 18.

(iv) A compound noun with a single stress, which from usage is regarded as one word, requires no hyphen, e.g. áirbus, bláckbird, dústman, fóotprint, néwspaper.

(v) Pronouns and adverbs beginning with any-, every-, and some-, are printed as single words in their conventional senses (anyone, everybody, etc.); as two separately stressed words each retains its own meaning (e.g. you can take any one of these books).

(vi) Many words in common use, originally printed as two words or hyphenated, are now used without the hyphen.

Examples:

aerofoil	byname	cotangent
airline	bypass	countdown
amidships	bypath	countryside
antenatal	bystander	crossword
antifreeze	byway	(*puzzle*)
antitetanus	byword	curvilinear
antitoxin	candlepower	disyllable
armchair	casework	downhill
arrowhead	catchword	electrolyte
battlefield	childbirth	electromotive
bloodstream	coalfield	electrostatic
blueprint	coaxial	endpaper
bookwork	coeducation	evermore
breakdown	coexistence	eyewitness
breakthrough	coextensive	fairyland
breakup	cornfield	farmyard
brickwork	cosecant	fatstock
bygone	cosine	feedback

filmsetting
firsthand, *a.*
flashback
flashpoint
flyleaf
flysheet
flywheel
folklore
foodstuff
footnote
footsore
footstool
freeboard
freshwater, *a.*
godlike
goodwill
grassland
grindstone
guidebook
halftone
hallmark
handbook
handlist
headmaster
headquarters
heartbeat
hillside
hilltop
horsepower
horseshoe
hundredweight
hydroelectric
indiarubber
interrelationship
keynote
kilogram
kilometre

ladybird
ladylike
landowner
lawcourt[1]
lawsuit
layout
letterhead
lifelike
lifelong
lifetime
livestock
loudspeaker
megawatt
microfilm
midbrain
midday
milestone
misspelling
monochrome
motorway
multiracial
nearby, *a.*
newcomer
newfangled
newsreel
noonday
notebook
offprint
offshoot
oilfield
onrush
outdoor
overall, *a., adv.,*
    and n.
overleaf
overnight, *a.*
    and adv.

overrule
paperback
particoloured
peacetime
photoelectric
polyethylene
polyvinyl
postcard
postnatal
racecourse
radioactive
rainfall
reappear[2]
reappraisal
reimburse
reinstate
reopen
reprint
resale
resell
roadside
runoff
runway
screenplay
seaplane
seaside
seaweed
selfsame
sidelight
sightseeing
smallpox
spaceship
spearhead
stepfather
stockpile
subcommittee
subnormal

[1] But the Law Courts.

[2] *re-* may be attached with a hyphen to a verb as a living prefix to distinguish the compound from a more familiar one-word form, e.g. re-cover (to cover again), re-form (to form again), re-pair (to pair again).

subscript	terracotta	wartime
subtitle	textbook	watercourse
subway	thermonuclear	wavelength
suchlike	today	wellnigh
supermarket	tomorrow	worthwhile
superscript	tonight	*(attrib.)*
tableland	twofold	wrongdoing
taxpayer	ultraviolet	wryneck
teenager	unselfconscious	zigzag

(vii) Many compound words having more than one stress require hyphens, e.g. cróss-quéstion, eásy-góing, shórt-térm. A hyphen is also usually desirable in a less familiar compound whose first element ends with a vowel and whose second element begins with a vowel, e.g. aero-elastic, radio-isotope, sea-urchin;[1] and where the first element ends with the same consonant as that beginning the second element, e.g. part-time.

(viii) A noun expressing the action of a verb and adverb usually takes a hyphen although the verbal form does not, e.g. change-over, hand-out, take-off.

Examples:

above-board	bile-duct	by-product
after-care	birth-control	by-road
aide-de-camp	birth-rate	calves-foot, *a.*
air-blast	blood-pressure	car-park
air-to-air	blood-supply	cat's-paw
ante-mortem, *a.*	body-weight	change-over
ante-post	boiler-room	chock-full
ante-room	boiling-point	colour-blind
Attorney-	book-plate	common-sense,
General	bull's-eye	*a.*
audio-visual	by-election	co-operate
back-bencher	by-law	co-ordinate[2]
bench-mark	by-play	copy-book

[1] More familiar words such as coeducation and radioactive are normally now printed without hyphens.

[2] Usually one word in mathematical works; note also uncoordinate.

corner-stone
court-martial, v.
cross-reference
cross-section
death-rate
de-ice
die-hard
ding-dong
drip-proof
ear-rings
engine-room
eye-muscles
fairy-tale
fall-out
far-fetched
filter-paper
freezing-point
gall-bladder
get-at-able
good-day
good-night
ground-level, a.
half-dozen
half-hour
half-past
half-title
half-way, a.
   and adv.
hand-out, n.
head-dress
head-note
heart-break
heart-broken
heat-content
hip-joint
hoar-frost

hymn-book
infra-red
internal-
   combustion, a.
jaw-bone
kick-off
knick-knack
know-how
lady-in-waiting
lamb's-wool
lay-by
litmus-paper
long-standing
looking-glass
look-out
love-affair
Major-General
man-of-war
melting-point
micro-organism
nerve-cell
non-co-operation
non-toxic
notice-board
oft-times
olive-oil
out-and-out
out-of-date[1]
out-of-doors[1]
physico-
   chemical
piezo-electric
place-name
pocket-book
post-mortem, n.
   and a.

post-war
pre-eminent
pre-war
pulse-rate
radio-carbon
record-player
re-entrant
sea-breeze
second-hand, a.
set-back
short-circuit, v.
son-in-law
starting-point
step-parent
strip-tease
swing-wing
   (aircraft)
take-off
take-over
test-tube
title-page
topsy-turvy
turning-point
twin-screw
up-country
up-to-date[1]
vice-consul
volt-ampere
wage-earner
water-colour
water-level
water-line
web-offset
well-being
work-piece
year-book[2]

(ix) Half an inch, half a dozen, etc. (with the article) require no hyphens. Print also without hyphens:

[1] When used attributively.
[2] But Year Book (reports) in law.

alpha ray
amino acid
beta ray
blood bank
blood cell
blood count
blood group
brake
  horsepower
business man
cast iron[1]
coat of arms
common sense[2]
court martial, *n.*
decimal point
easy chair
fellow men, etc.
flow rate
foot candle
for ever[3]
free will
  (*but* freewill
  offering)
gamma ray
gas poisoning
good humour

good nature
heat flow
high priest
high road
ill health
ill humour
ill luck
ill nature
ill will
income tax
in so far
mother tongue
motor car
near by, *adv.*
nickel silver
none the less
no one
Notary Public
oil well
on to
per cent
plum pudding
post mortem, adv.
post office
press reader
radium therapy

revenue office
Reynolds
  number (*no
  apostrophe*)
right angle
screw thread
sheet iron
short circuit, *n.*
square root
stop valve
stress rate
sweepback angle
trade union (*pl.*
  trade unions)
two and six
  (*in old cur-
  rency*)
twopence
  halfpenny
Union Jack
value added tax
wave number
worth while
  (*predic.*)
yield point

WORDS ENDING IN -ABLE AND -IBLE

WORDS ending in *-able* generally owe their form to the Latin termination *-abilis* or the Old French *-able* (or both), and words in *-ible* to the Latin *-ibilis*, e.g. durable from *durabilis* (*durare* to last), visible from *visibilis* (*videre* to see).

---

[1] But cast-iron when used attributively.

[2] But common-sense when used attributively.

[3] In sense 'for always'. Print as one word in sense 'continually', as in 'he is forever complaining'.

-able is also added to words of 'distinctly French or English origin' (*OED*, s.v. *-ble*), and as a living element to English roots, e.g. conceivable, movable, murderable, unget-at-able.

WORDS ENDING IN -ABLE

Alteration of the stem

(i) With some exceptions, words ending in silent *-e* lose the *e* when *-able* is added: adorable, excusable, indispensable.

Note, however, giveable, sizeable, and others in the list below; these are generally formed on words of one syllable in which loss of the final *e* would lead to ambiguity or excessive disguise of the root form.

(ii) Polysyllabic words ending in *-y* (as a simple syllable, not *-ay*, *-oy*, etc.) change *y* to *i*: dutiable, rectifiable, undeniable (*but* buyable, employable, flyable, payable).

(iii) In words ending in *-ce* or *-ge*, the *e* should be retained to preserve the soft sound of *c* or *g*: bridgeable, changeable, chargeable, noticeable, serviceable.

(iv) Words ending in *-ee* retain both letters: agreeable, feeable, foreseeable.

(v) Many verbs of more than two syllables ending in *-ate* drop this ending when forming adjectives in *-able*: alienable, calculable, demonstrable, penetrable, tolerable (*but* creatable, dictatable).

(vi) In words of English formation, a final consonant is usually doubled before *-able* when it is doubled in the present participle: conferrable,[1] forgettable, regrettable.

---

[1] But note inferable, preferable, referable, transferable.

Examples:

abominable	deferrable	impeccable
actionable	definable	imperturbable
adaptable	delineable	implacable
administrable	demonstrable	impressionable
admittable	demurrable	improvable
adorable	desirable	indefatigable
advisable	despicable	indescribable
agreeable	developable	indispensable
alienable	dilatable	indubitable
amenable	dissolvable	inflatable
amiable	drivable	inimitable
analysable	durable	insufferable
appreciable	dutiable	irreconcilable
arguable	eatable	irreplaceable
ascribable	educable	justifiable
assessable	endorsable	knowledgeable
atonable	equable	laughable
available	evadable	leviable
bearable	excisable	likeable
believable	excitable	liveable
blameable	excusable	losable
bribable	expendable	lovable
bridgeable	expiable	machinable
calculable	feeable	malleable
capable	finable	manageable
changeable	foreseeable	manœuvrable
chargeable	forgettable	marriageable
clubbable	forgivable	measurable
comfortable	framable	movable
conceivable	gettable	mutable
conferrable	giveable	nameable
confinable	hireable	noticeable
consolable	illimitable	objectionable
contractable[1]	immovable	obtainable
creatable	immutable	operable
curable	impalpable	palatable
datable	impassable (*that*	payable
debatable	*cannot be*	peaceable
declinable	*traversed*)	penetrable

[1] But contractible in the sense of restricting or shortening.

perishable
permeable
persuadable
pleasurable
preferable
prescribable
pronounceable
provable
rateable
readable
receivable
reconcilable
rectifiable
registrable

regrettable
reliable
removable
reputable
retractable
saleable
serviceable
sizeable
solvable
statutable
storable
suitable
superannuable
timeable

tolerable
traceable
tradable
transferable
tuneable
unconscionable
undeniable
unexceptionable
unget-at-able
unknowable
unmistakable
unscalable
unshakeable
usable

WORDS ENDING IN -IBLE

Examples:

accessible
adducible
admissible
audible
avertible
collapsible
comprehensible
contemptible
convertible
defensible
destructible
digestible
dirigible
discernible
divisible

eligible
expressible
extendible
feasible
flexible
gullible
impassible
  (*unfeeling*)
incorrigible
incredible
indelible
indigestible
infallible
intangible

irascible
irresistible
legible
negligible
ostensible
perceptible
permissible
persuasible
plausible
responsible
reversible
risible
susceptible
vendible

WORDS ENDING IN
-ISE, -IZE, AND -YSE

(i) Use *-ize* in preference to *-ise* as a verbal ending
in cases where both spellings are in use. Generally

corresponding to the Greek *-izo*, it is added to form
verbs to the stems of nouns ending in *-ism*, *-ization*,
-izer, *-y*, and to complete nouns. (For verbs in *-ize*
formed on proper names, such as galvanize, see
p. 13.)

Examples:

agony	agonize	criticism	criticize
appetizer	appetize	philosophy	philosophize
civilization	civilize	standard	standardize
colony	colonize	transistor	transistorize

For more recent formations of verbs in *-ize* see
Modern English Usage (2/e, 1965), s.v. *new verbs in
-ize*.

(ii) The ending *-ise* must be used when the verb
corresponds to a noun having *-is-* as part of the stem,
e.g. in the syllables *-vis-* (seeing, as in televise), *-cis-*
(cutting, as in excise), *-mis-* (putting, as in com-
promise), and when it is identical with a noun in
-ise, as in exercise, surprise.

(iii) Nouns with endings other than *-ism*, *-ization*,
-izer, and *-y*, such as those in *-ition* and *-ment*,
are not usually associated with verbs in *-ize* (or
-ise). Exceptions are aggrandizement/aggrandize,
recognition/recognize, and others noted in the
Concise Oxford Dictionary as 'assimilated to verbs
in *-ize*'. Reference should be made to *COD* and
the *Oxford Dictionary for Writers and Editors* in
doubtful cases.

Some of the more common verbs in *-ise* follow:

advertise	compromise	enterprise
advise	demise	(*chiefly in*
apprise	despise	*enterprising*)
arise	devise	excise
chastise	disguise	exercise
circumcise	emprise	improvise
comprise	enfranchise	incise

merchandise	promise	surmise
premise	revise	surprise
prise (open)	supervise	televise

(iv) *-ise* is also a termination of some nouns:

compromise	exercise	reprise
demise	expertise	surmise
disguise	franchise	surprise
enterprise	merchandise	

(v) In verbs such as analyse, catalyse, paralyse, *-lys-* is part of the Greek stem (corresponding to the element *-lusis*) and not a suffix like *-ize*. The spelling *-yze* is therefore etymologically incorrect, and must not be used, unless American printing style is being followed.

WORDS ENDING IN -MENT

T HE ending *-ment* is added to the complete verbal form, e.g. develop/development, excite/excitement. When the verb ends in *-dge*, the final *e* should be retained,[1] e.g. acknowledge/acknowledgement, judge/judgement (judgment is used as an exception in legal works).

[1] 'I protest against the unscholarly habit of omitting it from "abridgement", "acknowledgement", "judgement", lodgement", —which is against all analogy, etymology, and orthoepy, since elsewhere *g* is hard in English when not followed by *e* or *i*. I think the University Press ought to set a scholarly example, instead of following the ignorant to do ill, for the sake of saving four *e*'s. The word "judgement" has been spelt in the Revised Version correctly.' (Sir James Murray.)

DECIMAL CURRENCY

In British decimal currency, which was introduced on 15 February 1971, sums of money should be printed as follows:

Amounts in whole pounds: £2,542, £7.47 m.

Amounts expressed in new pence: 56p (no point) *not* £0·56

Mixed amounts of pounds and new pence: £24·74 *not* £24·74p

Amounts which include the new halfpenny should be expressed as a fraction: £12·45½; 7½p

There must always be two figures after the decimal point: £15·50; £15·07

Amounts expressed in £ s. d. will continue to be found in copy, which must be followed in the choice between £ s. d. and decimals.

Amounts in £ s. d. will naturally be found in:

(*a*) resetting books published before 1971, including all classics, and literature generally;

(*b*) quotations in new books from works (including letters and documents) dating from before 1971;

(*c*) new books in which the author is referring in his own words to events and conditions before 1971; e.g. 'In 1969 income tax stood at 8*s*. 3*d*. in the £'; 'My aunt gave me 3*s*. 6*d*. to buy a story-book.'

In categories (*b*) and (*c*) and in annotated editions of (*a*) it will be for the author or editor to decide, in future years, whether to introduce decimal equivalents of pre-1971 amounts for the benefit of those to whom shillings and pence are unfamiliar, or for ease of comparison (e.g. in statistics) with post-1971 figures.

RULES FOR SETTING
FOREIGN LANGUAGES

DUTCH AND AFRIKAANS

IJ ij developed out of *Ÿ ÿ*; they should be set one piece if possible, and not separated in letter-spacing; above all set *IJsselmeer* etc., not *Ij*-. The acute is used to distinguish *één* 'one' from *een* 'a', and *vóór* 'before' from *voor* 'for'; otherwise the only accent required (except in foreign loan-words) is the diaeresis: *knieën* 'knees', *provinciën* 'provinces', *zeeën* (seas), *zeeëend* 'marine duck'. Word-division is on the same lines as in German, but *s-t* is divided; consonant *+j* should be taken over. Punctuation is less strict than in German. When a word beginning with an apostrophe starts a sentence, it is the *following* word that takes the capital: *'t Is*.

This rule applies too in Afrikaans, where it is of great importance, since the indefinite article is written *'n*: thus *'n Man het gekom* 'A man has come'. There is no *ij* (*y* being used as in older Dutch); *s* is used at the start of words where Dutch has *z*, and *w* between vowels often where Dutch has *v*. The acute, grave, and circumflex are all used, the circumflex most frequently. Dutch *zeeën* is *seë* in Afrikaans, but after a *stressed* final *-ie* an *-ë* is added: *knieë*.

Note that since Afrikaans was not generally used in writing till the 1920s, books on early twentieth-century South Africa may quote the same phrases first in Dutch and later in Afrikaans; no query is required.

FRENCH

Abbreviations

SUCH words as article, chapitre, scène, titre, figure, are abbreviated only when in parentheses, as references; in the text they are put in full. The word premier (*or* première) is spelt out following such nouns (and after acte): Article premier, Art. 2.

Saint, sainte, when they occur very often, as in religious works, may be abbreviated, taking a capital letter: S. Louis, Ste Marie. But they are not abbreviated when they form part of a surname or place-name, e.g. Saint-Germain-des-Prés; in which case Saint- and Sainte- take a capital and are followed by a hyphen.[1] (See also p. 93.)

Contractions such as St, Ste, Mme, Mlle, etc., do not take the full point, the rule being that the full point is not placed after a contraction when the last letter of the word and the last letter of the contraction are the same.

The words monsieur, messieurs, madame, mesdames, monseigneur, messeigneurs, mademoiselle, mesdemoiselles, are written in full and all in lower case when not followed by a proper name: Oui, madame; Non, monsieur le duc; J'espère que monseigneur viendra;[2] J'ai vu monsieur votre père. Before names initial capitals are used: M. (for monsieur), Mme (for madame), Mgr (for monseigneur), etc. The words Sa Majesté, Son Éminence, Leurs Altesses, when followed by another title, are put as initials, thus S. M. l'Empereur; but not otherwise.

The name Jésus-Christ is abbreviated only after a date, thus: 337 avant J.-C. This is sometimes printed 337 av. J.-C.

---

[1] St-Germain, Ste-Catherine, St-Hilaire, la St-Jean, l'église de St-Sulpice are, however, met with in gazetteers, guide-books, etc.

[2] But, when referring to a third person: ...que M. Berthelot...

Other examples of abbreviations:

liv.	(livre)	p.	(page)
chap.	(chapitre)	p. *or* pp.	(pages)
t.	(tome)	P.-S.	(post-scriptum)
d^o	(dito)	etc.	(et cætera)
f^o	(folio)	c.-à-d.	(c'est-à-dire)
in-f^o	(in-folio)	Cie, Cie	(compagnie)
in-8°	(in-octavo)	Dr	(docteur)
in-4°	(in-quarto)	M.	(monsieur)
ms.	(manuscrit)	Me, M^e	(maître)
mss.	(manuscrits)	Mme, Mme	(madame)
n^o	(numéro)	Mlle, Mlle	(mademoiselle)
Ier, 1er (premier)		MM.	(messieurs)
IIe, 2e IIème, 2ème } (deuxième)		Vve	(veuve)

Abbreviations of metric units:

M	(méga = million)	a	(are)
mam	(myriamètre)	ca *or* m^2	(centiare)
km	(kilomètre)	das	(décastère)
hm	(hectomètre)	s *or* m^3	(stère)
dam	(décamètre)	ds	(décistère)
m	(mètre)	t	(tonne)
dm	(décimètre)	q	(quintal métrique)
cm	(centimètre)	kg	(kilogramme)
mc *or* m^3	(mètre cube)	hg	(hectogramme)
mq *or* m^2	(mètre carré)	dag	(décagramme)
mm	(millimètre)	g	(gramme)
mmq *or* mm^2	(millimètre	dg	(décigramme)
	carré)	cg	(centigramme)
mmc *or* mm^3	(millimètre cube)	mg	(milligramme)
ha	(hectare)	kl	(kilolitre)
hl	(hectolitre)	dl	(décilitre)
dal	(décalitre)	cl	(centilitre)
l	(litre)	ml	(millilitre)

Put: 20 francs, 20 mètres, 20 litres, 20 milli-grammes. If, however, followed by fractions, then put: 20 fr. 50 or 20^{fr},50; 20 m 50 or 20^m,50; 20 l 50 or 20^l,50.

The words kilogrammes, kilomètres, and kilogrammètres, followed by fractions, are given thus: 50 kg 3 or 50^{kg},3; 5 km 3 or 5^{km},3; 2 kgm 4 or 2^{kgm},4.

In works crowded with figures, one can even put: 0^m,5 for 5 décimètres; 0^m,15 for 15 centimètres; 0^m,008 for 8 millimètres.

The cubic metre followed by a fraction is given thus: 4^{mc},005 or 4^{m3},005 (= 4 mètres cubes 5 millimètres cubes); the square metre thus: 4^{mq},05 or 4^{m2},05 (= 4 mètres carrés 5 centimètres carrés).

The French use a decimal comma instead of a decimal point: 2,3 = 2.3.

Per cent is generally put 0/0, but pour 100, p. 100, and % are also used. In business letters pour cent is always pour %: à trente jours, 3 pour % d'escompte.

Accented capitals

With one exception accents are to be used with capital letters in French. The exception is the grave accent on the capital letter A in such lines as:

> A la porte de la maison, etc.;
> A cette époque, etc.;

and in display lines such as:

FÉCAMP A GENÈVE
MACHINES A VAPEUR

In these the preposition A takes no accent; but we must, to be correct, print Étienne, Étretat; and DÉPÔT, ÉVÊQUE, PRÉVÔT in cap. lines.[1] Small capitals, where used, should be accented in the same way as large capitals.

[1] There is no uniformity of practice in French printing-offices in regard to the accentuation of capital letters generally, although there is a consensus of opinion as to retaining accents for the letter E. The letter A, when a capital, standing for à, is never accented by French printers.

Awkward divisions: abbreviated words and large
numbers expressed in figures

One should avoid ending a line with an apostrophe,
such as: Quoi qu'|il dise.

If a number expressed in figures is too long to go
into a line, or cannot be taken to the next without
prejudice to the spacing, a part of the number should
be put as a word, thus: 100 mil-|lions.

Capital and lower case

In French surnames beginning with the feminine
article La should be given a capital: La Fontaine,
La Rochefoucauld; but the masculine article le with
the names of Italian writers and painters is written
lower case: le Tasse, l'Arioste, le Corrège.[1] Names
beginning de or de la take lower case in these words,
but Du and Des are found besides du and des. It is
advisable to consult *Le Petit Larousse* in case of
doubt. In place-names the article should have a
lower-case initial: le Mans, le Havre.

Numbers of volumes, books, titles, acts of plays,
the years of the Republican Calendar, are put in
large capitals: an IV, acte V, tome VI; also numerals
belonging to proper names: Louis XII; but not the
numbers of the arrondissements of Paris: le 15^e
arrondissement.

Numbers of scenes of plays, if there are no acts,
are also put in full capitals: *Les Précieuses ridicules*,
sc. V; also chapters if they form the principal
division: *Joseph*, ch. VI. If, however, scenes of plays
and chapters are secondary divisions, they are put
in small capitals: *Le Cid*, acte I, sc. II; *Histoire de
France*, liv. VI, ch. VII. The numbers of centuries

---

[1] 'Le Dante' for 'Dante' follows a mistake sometimes made
in Italian.

are generally put in small capitals: au xxe (*or* xxème) siècle.

The first word of a title takes an initial capital letter: *Les Femmes savantes*; *Le Monde*. However, where an author prefers lower-case *l* for the definite article (*le, la, les*) beginning a title, this style should be adopted; and the article may be construed with the surrounding sentence: les *Femmes savantes* sont le chef-d'œuvre de Molière. If a substantive in a title immediately follows *Le, La, Les*, it is also given a capital letter, thus: *Les Précieuses ridicules*. If such substantive is preceded by an adjective, this also receives an initial capital letter: *La Folle Journée*; if, however, the adjective follows, it has a lower-case initial: *L'Âge ingrat*. If the title commences with any other word than *le, la, les*, or an adjective, the words following are all in lower case unless they are proper nouns: *De la terre à la lune*; *Un lâche*.

In titles of fables and dramatic works names of the characters have capital initials: *Le Renard et les Raisins*; *Le Lion et le Rat*; *Marceau, ou les Enfants de la République*.

In catalogues or indexes having the first word(s) in parentheses after the noun commencing the line, the first word transposed has a capital letter: Homme (Faiblesse de l'); Honneur (L'); Niagara (Les Chutes du).

If the words in parentheses are part of the title of a work, the same rule is followed as to capitals as above given: *Héloïse* (*La Nouvelle*); *Mort* (*La Vie ou la*).

The words saint, sainte, when referring to the saints themselves, have, except when commencing a sentence, always lower-case initials: saint Louis, saint Paul, sainte Cécile. But when referring to place-names, feast-days, etc., capital letters and hyphens are used: Saint-Domingue, la Saint-Jean. (See also, as to abbreviations of saint, sainte, p. 89.)

I. Use capital letters as directed below:

(1) Words relating to God: le Seigneur, l'Être suprême, le Très-Haut, le Saint-Esprit.

(2) In enumerations, when each one commences a new line, a capital is put immediately after the ordinal figure:

> 1⁰ L'Europe.
> 2⁰ L'Asie, etc.

But when the enumeration is run on, lower-case letters are used: 1⁰ l'Europe, 2⁰ l'Asie, etc.

(3) The pronoun Elle referring to Votre Majesté, etc.

(4) The planets and constellations: la Terre, la Lune, Mars, le Bélier.

(5) Religious festivals: la Pentecôte.

(6) Historical events: la Révolution, la Réstauration, la Renaissance, l'Antiquité, la Réforme.

(7) The names of streets, squares, etc.: la rue des Mauvais-Garçons, la place de la Nation, la fontaine des Innocents.

(8) Names of public buildings, churches, etc.: l'Opéra, l'Odéon, Hôtel de Ville.

(9) Names relating to institutions, public bodies, religious, civil, or military orders (but only the word after the article): l'Académie française (but la Comédie-Française, le Théâtre-Français, and la Comédie-Italienne), la Légion d'honneur, le Conservatoire de musique.

(10) Surnames and nicknames, without hyphens: Louis le Grand.

(11) Honorary titles: Son Éminence, Leurs Altesses. But cf. p. 89 *ad fin.* for use of lower case when addressing a person.

(12) Adjectives in geographical expressions: la mer Rouge, le golfe Persique.

(13) The names of the cardinal points designating an extent of territory: l'Amérique du Nord; aller dans le Midi. See II (2).

(14) The word Église when it denotes the Church as an institution: l'Église catholique; but when relating to a building print église.

(15) The word État when it designates the nation, the country: La France est un puissant État. So too coup d'État.

(16) Persons of a nation and ages: les Anglais, les Anciens et les Modernes, les Français.

(17) Adjectives joined by hyphens to preceding nouns themselves with capitals: Comédie-Française, Comédie-Italienne.

II. Use lower-case initials for:

(1) The names of members of religious orders: un carme (a Carmelite), un templier (a Templar). But the names of the orders themselves take capitals: l'ordre des Templiers, des Carmes.

(2) The names of the cardinal points: le nord, le sud. But see I (13) above.

(3) Adjectives derived from proper names: la langue française, l'ère napoléonienne.

(4) Objects named from persons or places: un quinquet (an Argand lamp), un verre de champagne.

(5) Days of the week: lundi, mardi. Names of months: juillet, août.

(6) Members of religious sects, adherents of political movements (and their derivative adjectives): les juifs, les musulmans, chrétien(ne), calviniste, calvinisme, humaniste, protestant(e), jansénisme, janséniste, romantisme, romantique, socialisme, socialiste.

In plays the dramatis personae at the head of

scenes are put in large capitals, and those not named
in even small capitals:

SCÈNE V
TRIBOULET, BLANCHE, HOMMES,
FEMMES DU PEUPLE

In the dialogues the names of the speakers are put
in even small capitals, and placed in the centre of
the line. The stage directions and the asides are put
in smaller type,[1] and are in the text; if the play is in
verse, in parentheses over the words they refer to.
If there are two stage directions in one and the same
line, it will be advisable to split the line, thus:

(Revenu sur ses pas.)
Oublions-les! restons.— (Il l'assied sur un banc.)
            Sieds-toi sur cette pierre.

Directions not relating to any particular speaker
are set, if short, full right:

Celui que l'on croit mort n'est pas mort. — Le
    voici!   (Étonnement général.)

Dash

Dashes take a thin space before and after them; they
are never put close to a word like the English dash.
They are likewise never put after colons.

They are used to indicate conversational matter
(see below, *Quotation marks*), or to give more
force to a point: Il avait un cœur d'or, — mais une
tête folle; et vraiment, — je puis le dire, — il était
d'un caractère très agréable.

They are in addition used, as in English, for
parenthetical matter: Cette femme — étrangère sans
doute — était très âgée.

[1] Or in text italic.

Division of words

Words should be divided according to spoken
syllables, as in what the French call *épellation* (i.e.
syllabication), and in only a few cases according to
etymology. A single consonant always goes with the
following vowel (amou-reux, cama-rade), *ch*, *dh*, *gn*,
ph, *th*, and groups consisting of consonant+*r* or +*l*
counting as single consonants for this purpose (mé-
chant, Prou-dhon, ca-gneux, nénu-phar, Doro-thée,
pa-trie, ca-price, li-vraison); other groups are
divided irrespective of etymology (circons-tance,
tran-saction, obs-curité) except that a prefix is
detached before h (dés-habille). Note, however, that
ll is always divided even if sounded *y*: travail-lons.
Do not divide between vowels except in a compound
(extra-ordinaire but Moa-bite) nor before or after
an intervocalic *x* or *y*: soixante, moyen, are indivisible.

Compound words with internal apostrophe are
divided by pronunciation: s'en-tr'aimer, pres-qu'île,
aujour-d'hui, pru-d'homme. Note that compounds
of *grand* with feminine nouns have since 1932 been
spelt with a hyphen: grand-mère, not grand'mère.

In a narrow measure a syllable of two letters may
stand at the end of a line: ce-pendant, in-décis; but
a syllable of two letters must not be taken over to
the next line; therefore élégan-ce, adversi-té, are not
permissible; but élégan-ces, mar-que, abri-cot are
tolerated.

Avoid terminating a paragraph with only the final
syllable of a word in the last line.

Verbs taking the so-called euphonic *t* should always
be divided before the latter, thus: Viendra-|t-il?

Never divide abbreviated words, nor between or
after initials, nor after M., Mme, Mlle.

Mute syllables, provided they are of more than
two letters, may be turned over to the next line,

thus: ils don-nent, les hom-mes. Such divisions should however be avoided wherever possible.

Earlier spellings

Texts quoted from previous centuries may show spellings now obsolete: note especially the imperfect and conditional in *-ois -oit -oient*, and similarly françois anglois; the omission of *t* in the plural of such words as savant and événement; and the acute accent in the ending *-ége* now *-ège*: collége, Liége (used in Belgium till 1946), siége, etc. In the seventeenth century, when the classical literature of France was written, there were wider divergences from modern usage: desir for désir, pére for père, teste for tête, also portés for portez and vice versa. If an author reproduces the original spelling of a quoted work, his copy should be followed.

Hyphens

Place-names containing an article or the prepositions *en*, *de*, should have a hyphen between the component parts, thus: Saint-Germain-des-Prés, Saint-Valéry-en-Caux; but no hyphen between the introductory *le* or *la* and the noun in such names as la Ferté-Milon, la Ferté-sous-Jouarre.

Names of places, public buildings, or streets to which one or more distinguishing words are added usually take hyphens: Saint-Étienne-du-Mont, Vitry-le-François, rue du Faubourg-Montmartre, le Pont-Neuf, le Palais-Royal, but Hôtel des Monnaies. Distinguish Saint-Martin de Tours (the church of St Martin situated at Tours) and Saint-Martin-de-Laigle (where the name of the church is the same as that of the parish in which it is, or was, situated). Composite place-names are hyphenated, e.g. Saint-Denis-de-la-Réunion.

Hyphens are used to connect cardinal and ordinal

numbers in words under 100: e.g. vingt-quatre; trois
cent quatre-vingt-dix; but when *et* joins two numbers no hyphen is used, e.g. vingt et un; cinquante
et un, vingt et unième.

Note that certain classical names are regularly
written with hyphens: Marc-Antoine, Tite-Live,
Quinte-Curce, Marc-Aurèle, Aulu-Gelle; similarly
Jésus-Christ.

Compounds of né take the hyphen: nouveau-
né, un artiste-né.

Italic and roman type

In algebraical formulae the capital letters are always
put in roman and the small letters in italic. If,
however, the text is in italic, the small letters are put
in roman.

Titles of works, plays, and journals, names of
ships, of statues, and titles of tables mentioned in
the text, are put in italic; thus: La pièce *La Chatte
blanche*; J'ai vu *Les Rois en exil*; On lit dans le *Figaro*;
le journal *Le Temps*; le transport *Bien-Hoa*.

Foreign words and short quotations[1] are, as in
English, italicized: *Cave canem!* lisait-on...

Superior letters in words italicized should be in
italic, thus: *Histoire de Napoléon Ier*.

Numerals

When cardinal numbers were expressed in roman
lower-case letters, the final unit used to be expressed
by a j, not an i, thus: ij, iij, vj, viij.

Numbers are put in words if only occasionally
occurring in the text. If they are used statistically,
print them in figures.

Degrees of temperature are given thus: 15°, 15;
degrees of latitude and longitude, as in English,
15° 15′.

---

[1] That is, words foreign to French.

Age must be given in words, e.g. huit ans, and also times of day, if expressed in hours and fractions of hours, e.g. six heures, trois heures et quart. But time expressed in minutes, e.g. 6 h. 15 m. or 6 h. 00 m., should be set in figures.

Dates, figures, etc., are put in words in legal documents: l'an mil neuf cent quatre (the year one thousand nine hundred and four).

In figures middle spaces are used to divide thousands, thus: 20 250 fr. 25 or 20 250^{fr},25. But dates, and numbers in general, are always put without a space: l'an 1466; page 1250; Code civil, art. 2000.

One should not put 'de 5 à 6 000 hommes', but 'de 5 000 à 6 000 hommes'.

Fractions with a horizontal stroke are preferred in mathematical and scientific works; but in ordinary works the diagonal stroke can be used, thus: 1/2, 2/3 ($\frac{1}{2}$, $\frac{2}{3}$).

In logarithm tables the fractional part of a logarithm is printed with spaces, thus: Log. 2670 = 3, 426 5113; and also: Log. 2670 = 3, 4 265 113.

Punctuation

In general, French punctuation is rhetorical, not logical, and tends to be lighter than English: e.g. commas are often used where English would have colons or semicolons, and the comma is omitted before 'et' in enumerations. However, the comma is more freely used than in English to set off an adverbial phrase at the beginning of a sentence: Sur la rivière, on voyait un bateau. The space of the line should be set before a colon.

Quotation marks

In books (including lectures) completely in French use special quotation marks « » (called guillemets).

A guillemet is repeated at the head of every subsequent paragraph belonging to the quotation.

In conversational matter guillemets are sometimes put at the beginning and end of the remarks, and the individual utterances are denoted by a dash (spaced). But it is more common to dispense with guillemets altogether, and to denote the speakers by a dash only. This is an important variation from the English method.

If the » comes after 'points de suspension' (see p. 103), a thin space is put before it:

La cour a décrété qu' «attendu l'urgence...»

If, in dialogue, a passage is quoted, the « is put before the dash:

«— Demain, à minuit, nous sortirons enfin!»

In tables and workings the » is used to denote an absent quantity:

| 125 . 15 | 130 » |
| 10 » | 15 . 25 |

When a sentence contains a quotation, the punctuation mark at the end of the latter is put before the », and the mark belonging to the sentence after:

«Prenez garde au chien!», lisait-on à l'entrée des maisons romaines.

If the matter quoted ends with a full stop, and a comma follows in the sentence, the full stop is suppressed:

«C'est par le sang et par le fer que les États grandissent», a dit Bismarck.

Also, if the point at the end of the quotation is a full stop, and the sentence ends with a question or exclamation mark, the full stop is suppressed:

A-t-il dit: «Je reviendrai»?

When quotation and sentence end with the same point, only the quotation is pointed:

Quel bonheur d'entendre : « Je vous aime! »
A-t-il dit : « Qui est ici? »
Il a dit : « Je viendrai. »

But if the punctuation at the end of the quotation differs from that of the sentence, both points are put unless the sentence would take a full point:

A-t-il dit : « Quel grand malheur! »?
but Il a dit : « Quel grand malheur! »

Put before opening and after closing guillemets the space of the line, and thin spaces inside them.

In a quotation within a quotation, the « must stand at the commencement of each line of the enclosed quotation:

On lit dans *le Radical*: « Une malheureuse erreur a été commise par un de nos artistes du boulevard. Ayant à dire: « Mademoiselle, je ne veux qu'un mot de vous! », il a fait entendre ces paroles: « Mademoiselle, je ne veux qu'un « mou de veau! »

When every line begins with a guillemet, put a thin space after the « commencing each line.

Only one » is put at the end of two quotations ending simultaneously.

Reference figures

References to notes are generally rendered thus: (1), or thus: [1]. Sometimes an asterisk between parentheses (*) or standing alone *, or italic superior letter ([a]), is used. Superior figures not enclosed in parentheses are the best from the English point of view. In books or articles written in French, these figures should precede any mark of punctuation.

The figure in the note itself is put either 1. or (1) or [1]. In many works the reference figure is put [1], and the note figure 1.

Spacing

No spaces are to be put before the 'points de suspension', i.e. three points close together, cast in one piece, denoting an interruption (...). Section-marks, daggers, and double daggers take a thin space before or after them. Asterisks and superior figures, not enclosed in parentheses, referring to notes, usually take a thin space before them. Points of suspension are always followed by a space. For guillemets see pp. 100 ff.

A space is put after an apostrophe following a word of two or more syllables (as the French reckon syllables, e.g. bonne is a word of two syllables):

Bonn' petite...

Spaces are put in such a case as 10 h. 15 m. 10 s. (10 hours 15 min. 10 sec.), also printed 10^h 15^m 10^s.

GERMAN

A useful reference-book for German spelling and style of printing is Duden, *Rechtschreibung der deutschen Sprache und der Fremdwörter*, 15. Auflage, Mannheim, 1961, Bibliographisches Institut AG.

ROMAN (*Antiqua*) type is now normally used in German-speaking countries; but German types (*Fraktur* and *Schwabacher*) are still used to a limited extent in Germany both for bookwork and for jobbing.

German sorts in roman type. In addition to the roman alphabet used in England, the following extra sorts are required for the German language: the vowels with the mark for an *Umlaut* Ä, Ö, Ü, ä, ö, ü, and the *Eszett* ß.[1] The combinations ch, ck, and tz, sometimes provided by German type-founders with roman types, need not be used. The

---

[1] There are no corresponding capital and small capital letters for ß: and SS and ss are used.

ligatures ffi and ffl should NOT be used in setting
German. Use 2-piece fl in Auflage; 1-piece fl
in Aufl.

Sorts in German type. The following are the sorts
normally provided in *Fraktur* types with their
roman equivalents:

𝔄 𝔄 𝔅 ℭ 𝔇 𝔈 𝔉 𝔊 ℌ ℑ 𝔎 𝔏 𝔐 𝔑 𝔒 𝔒 𝔓 𝔔 ℜ
A Ä B C D E F G H I *or* J K L M N O Ö P Q R

𝔖 𝔗 𝔘 𝔘 𝔙 𝔚 𝔛 𝔜 ℨ
S T U Ü V W X Y Z

a ä b c d e f g h i j k l m n o ö p q r ſ s t u ü v w
a ä b c d e f g h i j k l m n o ö p q r s s t u ü v w

x y z ch ck ff fi fl ll si ſſ st ß tz
x y z ch ck ff fi fl ll si ss st ß tz

Abbreviations

The customary German abbreviations are followed
by full points, and thin spaces are put after full
points within them. Examples are: a. a. O. (am ange-
führten Ort), Dr. (Doktor), Frl. (Fräulein), usw.
(und so weiter).

The abbreviations for metric measures and
weights are not followed by full points: mm, cm, m,
qm or m^2, cbm or m^3; l, hl; g, kg, dz, t (see list in
French section, p. 90).

A number of abbreviations of recent origin are set
in capital letters and are not followed by full points:
e.g. AG (Aktiengesellschaft), BRD (Bundesrepublik
Deutschland), DDR (Deutsche Demokratische Re-
publik), HO (Handelsorganisation), DM (Deutsche
Mark); note too GmbH (Gesellschaft mit be-
schränkter Haftung).

In German texts print figures in full, using em
not en rule: 27—28, 331—335. ·

Accented letters

It is permissible to use roman accented letters and letters with cedilla with German type when setting foreign words (e.g. Café, Alençon).

Apostrophe

The apostrophe is used to mark the elision of *e* to render colloquial usage: e.g. Wie geht's, ich komm'; but not if the elision has been accepted in literary language: e.g. unsre, die andren. Thus in the present indicative ich lass', but imperative laß! When the apostrophe occurs at the beginning of a sentence, the following letter does not therefore become a capital: 's brennt (*not* 'S brennt).

It is also used to mark the suppression of the possessive *s* (for reasons of euphony) after names ending in s, ß, x, z: Voß' Luise, Demosthenes' Reden, Aristoteles' Werke, Horaz' Oden.

Article and book titles

These are set in roman (or, in a *Fraktur* text, in *Fraktur*) and often without quotation marks. This does not apply to German titles quoted within an English text, which should follow the style laid down on pp. 50 ff.

Borrowed words

In texts set in *Fraktur*, foreign words not assimilated into German are usually set in roman: sie kommen in corpore. In texts set in roman, however, it is not normal to set them in italic.

Division of words

Avoid dividing words of one syllable or turning over fewer than three letters to the next line. Simple (as opposed to compound) words should be divided by syllables, either between consonants: e.g. Fin-ger, fal-len, An-ker, Red-ner, war-ten; or after a vowel followed by a single consonant: e.g. lo-ben, tra-gen, Va-ter. This applies even to x and mute h: Bo-xer, verge-hen. When a division has to be made between three or more consonants, the last should be turned over: e.g. Vermitt-ler, Abwechs-lung, Derff-linger, kämp-fen, kämpf-ten. But certain combinations of consonants must not be separated: these are ch, ph, sch, ß, th (representing single sounds), and st. Correct examples are: spre-chen, wa-schen, So-phie, ka-tholisch, La-sten, Fen-ster, wech-seln, Wechs-ler. If ss is used instead of ß, it should be taken over entire: genie-ssen = genie-ßen, but ss not standing for ß should be divided: las-sen. For historical reasons, if a word is broken at the combination ck, it is represented as though spelt with kk: thus Zucker, but Zuk-ker; Glocken, but Glok-ken. However, in proper names or their derivatives, ck after a consonant is taken over bodily: Fran-cke, bismar-ckisch.

For this purpose words with suffixes are considered as simple words and divided in accordance with the rules given above: Bäcke-rei, le-bend, Liefe-rung.

Compound words may be broken into their etymological constituents: e.g. Bildungs-roman, Bürger-meister, Haus-frau, Kriminal-polizei, strom-auf, Zwillings-bruder, Bundes-tag (the rule against dividing st does not apply at the point of junction in compounds); and prefixes may be separated from the root-word: e.g. ge-klagen, emp-fehlen, er-obern, aus-trinken, ab-wechseln, zer-splittern. Note that it is quite permissible to divide a compound within one of its elements; Bun-destag is no less correct than Bundes-tag, and should be preferred if it gives better spacing. Words from the classical languages are sometimes divided according to classical rules; for the details see Duden.

Three identical consonants are not written before a vowel, although they sometimes occur before another consonant: stickstofffrei *but* Brennessel, Schiffahrt; but when a word is broken, the element turned over recovers its initial consonant: Brenn-nessel, Schiff-fahrt. The divisions Mit-tag, den-noch, and Drit-teil are exceptions.

Hyphens

Compound words are written both with and without hyphens in German, as in English; a noun after a hyphen commences with an initial capital: Mozart-Konzertabend, Schiller-Museum, Bet-Tuch (prayer-shawl). The Duden form should be followed. When part of a compound word is omitted to save repetition, the hyphen is used to mark the suppression: e.g. Feld- und Gartenfrüchte, ein- und ausatmen. In this case the hyphen is followed by the space of the line (or preceded by it, as in Jugendlust und -leid). The hyphen is used to avoid the double repetition of a vowel, e.g. Kaffee-Ersatz, but not to avoid the similar repetition of a consonant, e.g. stickstofffrei.

Initial capitals

All nouns in German are written with initial capital letters. Adjectives, numerals, and the infinitives of verbs are also given initial capitals if used as nouns: Gutes und Böses; die Drei; Sagen und Tun ist zweierlei. The pronouns Sie and Ihr have capitals when they mean 'you' and 'your'; likewise Du, Dein, Ihr, and Euer in letters, and Ihr, Euer, Er, etc., in older usage as pronouns of address to a single person. Adjectives have initial capitals when forming part of a geographical name, e.g. Kap der Guten Hoffnung,

Schwarzes Meer, or the names of historic events or eras, e.g. die Französische Revolution (of 1789), der Dreißigjährige Krieg, have initial capitals. German adjectives derived from personal names are given initial capitals when they are used to denote only association with the person from whose name they derive, e.g. die Grimmschen Märchen (*Grimm's Fairy Tales*), die Lutherische Bibelübersetzung (Luther's translation of the Bible); but when they are used in a more general sense, the initial capital is dropped, e.g. die lutherische Kirche (the Lutheran Church), ein napoleonischer Unternehmungsgeist (a Napoleonic spirit of enterprise). Adjectives denoting nationality have no initial capitals: das deutsche Vaterland; die italienische Küste. The word 'von' in personal names is written with a lower-case initial, but with a capital at the beginning of a sentence unless it is abbreviated to v., when a lower-case initial is used to avoid confusion with the initial of a Christian name.

Letter-spacing for emphasis

Letter-spacing is the means adopted for emphasizing words in *Fraktur* type (as italic is used for emphasis in English practice). When setting roman, German printers use letter-spacing or italic or small capitals for emphasis. In letter-spaced matter spaces are put before the punctuation marks excepting the full point. The combinations ch, ck, tz are to be regarded as single letters, and must not be spaced apart; this does not apply to ch, ck, and tz in roman unless so requested.

Ligatures

The ligatures ff, fi, and fl must not be used for all combinations of these letters, but only as follows. Set them where the letters belong together in the

stem of a word: treffen, finden, flehen; set fl finally
(Aufl.) and fi where i begins a suffix (häufig); note
that fi then takes precedence over ff: pfäffisch.
Otherwise use the separate letters: auffällen,
Schilfinsel, verwerflich (so too Auflage despite
Aufl.), i.e. where the letters link elements in a compound, or at the junction of a prefix or of a suffix
beginning with l. Note too that fl should be set
separately in words that have related forms with
-fel-: zweifle from zweifeln, Mufflon from Muffel.
In foreign compounds set Offizier, Effluvium; but
in the proper name Effi use ff. In *Fraktur* these
rules apply also to the ligatures ll (fallen but regellos),
ſi, and ſſ (lauſig, ruſſiſch like häufig, pfäffiſch). Note
that ſi, ſſ, ß, and ſt must not be used across a junction: ausimpfen, ausſehen, ausziehen, austauſchen.
Likewise ß must not be used in achtzig (contrast
trotzig from Trotz) or Achtzahl. Whenever there is
any doubt, set separate letters. (Some German
houses do not use ligatures in roman at all.)

Numerals

A number of more than four figures should be separated in thousands by thin spaces: e.g. 6 580 340.
The comma in German practice marks the decimal point (it is used in writing amounts of money
in decimal coinage: e.g. 15,00 DM, or 0,75 DM). A
full point after a numeral shows that it represents
an ordinal number: e.g. 14. Auflage (14th edition);
Friedrich II. von Preußen; Mittwoch, den 18. Juli
1956. The full point also marks the separation of
hours from minutes: e.g. 14.30 Uhr.

Punctuation

German practice differs from English in several
respects. Subordinate clauses of whatever kind are
marked off from main clauses by commas and so are

most infinitive or participial phrases (but not such
encapsulations as der von dieser Firma getriebene
Handel); note that if daß is preceded by a conjunction, the comma is set before the conjunction:
e.g. Ich höre, daß du nichts erspart hast, sondern
daß du sogar noch die Ersparnisse deiner Frau
vergeudest. Er beeilte sich, so daß er den Zug noch
erreichte. Two clauses linked by und or oder do
not take a comma between them unless they are
main clauses each with its subject indicated. For
further details see Duden.

Sentences containing an imperative normally end
in the mark of exclamation; the older practice by
which the salutation in a letter so ended (Sehr
geehrter Herr Schmidt!) is giving way to the use of
a comma, after which the letter proper does *not* begin
with a capital unless one is otherwise required.

Square brackets are used for parentheses within
parentheses. Em rules (and longer rules) are preceded and followed by spaces.

Quotation marks

German quotation marks take the form of two
commas at the beginning of the quotation, and two
turned commas at the end. Quotations within
quotations are marked by a single comma at the
beginning and a turned comma at the end. The
quotation marks are not separated by spaces from
the quotation. Punctuation following a quotation is
put after the closing quotation mark. French
guillemets, but pointing inwards (» «), are now
preferred by some German printers to the traditional
German quotation marks.

Use of ſ and ß

The long ſ is used in setting *Fraktur* type at the
beginnings of words, and within them except at the
ends of syllables. The short final -s is put at the ends

of syllables and words (see Duden). By way of
exception, in *Fraktur* type the long ſ is used at the
ends of syllables before p (Wespe, Knospe) and in ſſ.
The ß or ß is not divided when words are broken
at the ends of lines: e.g. hei=ßen, genie-ßen. It is used
at the end of a syllable, or before a consonant, whatever the vowel, but before a vowel only after a long
vowel or diphthong: thus Fuß in the plural makes
Füße but Kuß makes Küsse; Meßopfer but Messe;
ihr eßt, ihr aßt, but wir essen vs. wir aßen. Except
in capitals, ss should not be substituted for ß;
and ſſ must never be used for ß in *Fraktur*. Note
that in alphabetical order ß ß counts as ss, and not
sz; also that some personal names are spelt with ss
instead of ß by their bearers' wish.

GREEK AND LATIN

THE Greek alphabet consists of twenty-four letters
—seventeen consonants and seven vowels. The
vowels are: a, ϵ, η, ι, o, v, ω.

The following is the order of the letters:

A	α	alpha	N	ν	nu
B	β	beta	Ξ	ξ	xi
Γ	γ	gamma	O	o	omicron
Δ	δ	delta	Π	π	pi
E	ϵ	epsilon	P	ρ	rho
Z	ζ	zeta	Σ	σ	(ς final) or C c sigma
H	η	eta	T	τ	tau
Θ	θ	theta	Y	v	upsilon
I	ι	iota	Φ	ϕ	phi
K	κ	kappa	X	χ	chi
Λ	λ	lambda	Ψ	ψ	psi
M	μ	mu	Ω	ω	omega

The forms C c (lunate sigma) are preferred by
some authors. In reproducing inscriptions and

dialectal forms the letters Ϝ ϝ (wau or digamma) and Ϙ ϙ (koppa) are used, and also italic *h*; see also below, *Numbers*.

The vowels α η ω may occur with the letter iota beneath them ('subscript') ᾳ ῃ ῳ; some authors prefer to write αι ηι ωι ('adscript iota'), in which case accents and breathings should be set on the first vowel.

In texts of papyri and inscriptions any letter, with or without breathing, accent, or iota subscript, may be required to have a dot beneath it.

Aspirates and accents

᾽	Lenis (smooth)	῍	Asper grave
῾	Asper (rough)	ᾶ	Circumflex
´	Acute	᾽̑	Circumflex lenis
`	Grave	῾̑	Circumflex asper
῎	Lenis acute	¨	Diaeresis
῍	Lenis grave	΅	Diaeresis acute
῝	Asper acute	῭	Diaeresis grave

The acute (´) is only used upon one of the last three syllables of a word.

The grave (`) can only be used upon the last syllable of a word.

The circumflex (ˆ) occurs upon either the last syllable of a word, or the last but one.

The Greek vowels allow of two breathings: the asper or rough ('), corresponding to the letter *h*; and the lenis or smooth ('), which denotes the absence of the *h*.

All vowels beginning a word have a breathing over them; but upsilon (υ) allows of no other than the asper. In diphthongs (αι not standing for ᾳ, ει, οι, υι, αυ, ευ, ηυ, ου, ωυ) the breathing stands over the second vowel (thus: αἱ, οὐ) as do accents.

The initial letter ρ takes the asper.

Double ρρ was formerly printed ῥῤ ('horns'), but should now always be ρρ.

The lenis (') is used for eliding the vowels
α, ε, ι, ο, and sometimes the diphthongs αι and οι,
when they stand at the end of a word or syllable,
followed by another vowel beginning a word or
syllable. Elision takes place in all the prepositions,
except περί and πρό.

An elided word is not set close up with the word
following and may be set at the end of a line even
if it contains only one consonant and the lenis
('apostrophe'): δ'.

When there is fusion of two syllables, the breathing
is on the fused vowel or diphthong, the aspirate
becoming 'smooth' when the first consonant takes
the 'rough' breathing of the second word; e.g.
τὸ ἐπί = τοὐπί; τὸ ἱμάτιον = θοἰμάτιον; καὶ ἡ = χἠ;
πρό + ἔχω = προὔχω. The lenis here is called a
'coronis'.

The diaeresis (¨) is used to separate two vowels
from each other, and to prevent their being taken
for a diphthong.

Note the following rules: no word can have an
accent except over one of the last three syllables; the
grave (`) over the last syllable of a word; and the
asper grave (῍) and *lenis grave* (῏) over a few mono-
syllables.

The majority of words in the Greek language have
an *accent*, and rarely have more than one; when this
occurs, it is an *acute* thrown back upon the last
syllable from an enclitic, which is not accented except
when it is followed by another enclitic. No word can
have an *acute* accent over the last syllable except
in this case, or before a comma, full point, colon,
or interrogation, when the *grave* is changed to an
acute.

When a Greek word accented grave on its last
syllable appears in an English context and is followed by English words, its grave accent is changed
to acute.

Capitals

It is not normal to start a sentence or a line of verse in Greek texts with a capital, except in proper names; in Latin a capital may be used to introduce a sentence but need not be (follow copy), but lines of verse begin with lower case.

Division of words

Usually a vowel can be divided from another:

be-atus, λύ-ων

but some combinations form one sound, a diphthong, one syllable only:

ae, au, eu, oe, αι, αυ, ει, ευ, ηυ, οι, ου, υι

and these must not be divided.

In Greek, take over any combination of 'mute' (β γ δ θ κ π τ φ χ) followed by 'liquid' (λ μ ν ρ), also βδ γδ κτ πτ φθ χθ, or any of these followed by ρ; μν; and any group in which σ stands before a consonant other than σ, or before one of the above groups; in Latin the grammarians decree that these groups as transliterated shall be taken over even in native words. Examples:

ct- and κτ- (ctenoid)	fa-ctus, ἑλι-κτός
gn-, γν- (gnomon)	di-gnus, γι-γνώ-σκω
mn-, μν- (mnemonic)	da-mnum, μι-μνή-σκω
pn-, πν- (pneumonia)	hy-pnotice, κα-πνός
ps-, (ψ-) (psychology)	la-psus, (ἀνε-ψιός)
pt-, πτ- (ptomaine, Ptolemy)	sum-ptus, βα-πτί-ζω

Any doubled consonants may be divided; also, apart from the above exception for m (μ), the letters l, m, n, and r (Greek λ, μ, ν, and ρ) may be divided from a following consonant.

In Greek γ may be divided from a following κ or χ. Greek ξ and Latin x between vowels should be taken over (δεί-ξειν, pro-ximus) except as below.

The above rules are subject to the overriding rule that compound words are divided into their parts. It would help the compositor to be alert to the following prefixes ending in consonants:

ab, ad, ex, ob, red, sub, εἰσ, ἐν, ἐξ, ἐσ, ξυν, προσ,[1] συν.

Usually a division after these, even before a vowel, will be correct.

In Greek ἀντι-, ἀπο-, ἐπι-, κατα-, μετα-, παρα-, ὑπο- have their full form before a word-part beginning with a consonant: then divide as usual:

$$\mathit{ἀπο\text{-}κνίζω, κατα\text{-}λύω.}$$

But before a word-part beginning with a vowel (or aspirated vowel) they become ἀντ- (ἀνθ-), ἀπ- (ἀφ-), ἐπ- (ἐφ-), κατ- (καθ-), μετ- (μεθ-), παρ-, ὑπ- (ὑφ-), and then it will be right to divide after the consonant:

$$\mathit{ἀπ\text{-}αίρω, καθ\text{-}ήκω.}$$

There are some other cases, chiefly compound words, where a more detailed knowledge of the language must decide.[2] The instances where the foregoing rules do not suffice will be few and can be left to specialist readers to adjust.

So, too, may those instances where the vowel of a preposition is cut off before the identical vowel. For example:

ὀκνῶ is a simple word: therefore ἀπ-οκνῶ is correct.

ἅπτομαι is a simple word: therefore παρ-άπτομαι is correct.

---

[1] But note that there is also a prefix προ- which may occur before σ.

[2] e.g. hac-tenus, non-iam, red-ibo, sol-ueret, Ἀλέξ-ανδρος, δήμ-αρχος, Διοσ-κόρω, ὥσπερ-ανεί are correct divisions.

Numerals

1	α′	18	ιη′	500	φ′
2	β′	19	ιθ′	600	χ′
3	γ′	20	κ′	700	ψ′
4	δ′	21	κα′	800	ω′
5	ε′	22	κβ′	900	⟩′
6	ϛ′	23	κγ′	1,000	͵α
7	ζ′	30	λ′	2,000	͵β
8	η′	40	μ′	3,000	͵γ
9	θ′	50	ν′	4,000	͵δ
10	ι′	60	ξ′	5,000	͵ε
11	ια′	70	ο′	6,000	͵ϛ
12	ιβ′	80	π′	7,000	͵ζ
13	ιγ′	90	ϟ′	8,000	͵η
14	ιδ′	100	ρ′	9,000	͵θ
15	ιε′	200	σ′	10,000	͵ι
16	ιϛ′	300	τ′	20,000	͵κ
17	ιζ′	400	υ′	100,000	͵ρ

ϛ and ⟩ are nowadays called 'stigma' and 'sampi' respectively.

In modern Greek arabic numerals are used: set these in italic with Porson, but roman with Hellenic, in both cases ranging.

Punctuation

In Greek the comma, the full point, and the exclamation (in modern Greek) are the same as in English; but the question mark (;) is the English semicolon (italic where necessary to match the Greek fount being used), and the colon is an inverted full point (·).

Use double quotes generally in Greek.

Spacing

In Greek emphasized words should be letter-spaced.

ITALIAN

THE use of accents in the Italian language is not entirely consistent; as a general rule follow the author's manuscript.

Division of words

The following compound consonants are not to be divided: bl, br; ch, cl, cr; dr; fl, fr; gh, gl, gn, gr; pl, pr; sb, sc, sd, sf, sg, sl, sm, sn, sp, sq, sr, st, sv; tl, tr; vr; sbr; sch; scr; sdr; sfr; sgh; sgr; spl; spr; str. Divide between vowels only if neither is i or u.

When the vowel is followed by a doubled consonant, the first of these goes with the vowel, and the second is joined to the next syllable; i.e. the division comes between the two letters: lab-bro, mag-gio. So also ac-qua, nac-que, noc-que, piac-que—these are really doubled consonants.

In the middle of a word, if the first consonant of a group is a liquid (i.e. either *l*, *m*, *n*, or *r*) it makes a syllable with the preceding vowel, and the other consonant, or combination of consonants, goes with the succeeding vowel: al-tero, ar-tigiano, tem-pra.

In words which have the prefixes *as-*, *es-*, *dis-*, *tras-*, the words are divided so as to separate the entire prefix: as-trarre, es-posto, dis-fatta, tras-porto. If assimilation has taken place, we have, according to the foregoing rules, ef-fluvio, dif-ficile, dif-fuso.

Divide dal-l'aver, sen-z'altro, quaran-t'anni; cf. next paragraph.

Spacing

In Italian put the ordinary spacing of the line after an apostrophe following a vowel (and in this case when necessary the apostrophe may end a line); but there should be no space after an apostrophe following a consonant (in this case the apostrophe may not end a line): e.g. *a' miei, de' malevoli, i' fui, ne' righi, po' duro*; but *dall'aver, l'onda, s'allontana, senz'altro*. (Note that where an apostrophe replaces a vowel at the beginning of a word a space always precedes it, e.g. *e 'l, su 'l, te 'l, che 'l.*)

ORIENTAL LANGUAGES IN ROMAN TYPE

THE principal Oriental languages have alphabets of their own.

Often words or sentences in these languages have to be set up in roman type. But there is as yet no uniform fixed system of spelling words from any of these languages when set in roman. Therefore the system used in the copy should generally be followed as far as possible. Note the frequent use of under-lined letters: e.g. Arabic ث may be transliterated t or th.

In Semitic languages 'ain and hamza/'aleph are to be represented by a Greek asper and a lenis respectively.

Examples: 'ain (asper) 'ālim, mu'allim, ḍā'.

hamza (lenis) 'amīr, mu'allim, ḍā'.

In each case the sign is to be treated as a letter of the alphabet and part of the word and must not be confused with a quotation mark. Note that an apostrophe, denoting elision, usually appears before l followed by a hyphen, e.g. 'Abdu 'l-Malik. (NB. The turned comma is not to be used for 'ain unless specially ordered.)

In printing Arabic, etc., long vowels are to be represented by a stroke, not a circumflex, unless otherwise ordered: tawārīkh, not tawârîkh; ma'lūm, not ma'lûm.

In printing Ancient Egyptian words in roman type use the special sign ˁ (capital), ˁ (lower case) instead of the Greek asper '. Note that this and the other special letters ꜣ ꞽ 'I ỉ have their own italic forms ˁ ˁ ꜣ ꞽ 'I ỉ.

RUSSIAN

THESE notes relate specifically to questions of orthography, punctuation, and typography which may arise when editing or setting matter in Russian.[1] *They are in principle restricted to points where English and Russian practice diverge.*

It should be stressed that many points cannot be fully covered by formal rules: a knowledge of Russian word-formation and syntax is often essential if correct decisions are to be reached in individual cases.

Russian is one of the six Slavonic languages that are written in Cyrillic script—the others being (in the USSR) Belorussian (or White Russian) and Ukrainian, and (outside the USSR) Bulgarian, Macedonian, and Serbian. The additional sorts called for by the five non-Russian languages are omitted from the table of the Cyrillic alphabet which follows, but details of them are given in the text below it.

Additional sorts (including those eliminated in 1918) are used when setting Old Russian texts; Old Church Slavonic also calls for additional sorts, and is usually set in a face which bears the same relation to modern Russian types as black letter does to normal roman faces.

The table includes 'upright' (*pryamoĭ*) and 'cursive' (*kursiv*) forms and also a transliteration in accordance with the 'British System' as given in British Standard 2979:1958. For further information about transliteration see *Transliteration*.

---

[1] For fuller information see, in general, L. A. Gil′berg and L. I. Frid, *Slovar′-spravochnik avtora* (Moscow, 1979), and, for orthography, see K. I. Bylinskiĭ and N. N. Nikol′skiĭ, *Spravochnik po orfografii i punktuatsii dlya rabotnikov pechati*, 4th edn. (Moscow, 1970).

А	а	*А*	*а*	a	Р	р	*Р*	*р*	r
Б	б	*Б*	*б*	b	С	с	*С*	*с*	s
В	в	*В*	*в*	v	Т	т	*Т*	*т*	t
Г	г	*Г*	*г*	g	У	у	*У*	*у*	u
Д	д	*Д*	*д*	d	Ф	ф	*Ф*	*ф*	f
Е	е	*Е*	*е*	e	Х	х	*Х*	*х*	kh
Ё	ё	*Ё*	*ё*	ë[1]	Ц	ц	*Ц*	*ц*	ts
Ж	ж	*Ж*	*ж*	zh	Ч	ч	*Ч*	*ч*	ch
З	з	*З*	*з*	z	Ш	ш	*Ш*	*ш*	sh
И	и	*И*	*и*	i	Щ	щ	*Щ*	*щ*	shch
Й	й	*Й*	*й*	ĭ	Ъ	ъ	*Ъ*	*ъ*	"
К	к	*К*	*к*	k	Ы	ы	*Ы*	*ы*	ȳ
Л	л	*Л*	*л*	l	Ь	ь	*Ь*	*ь*	'
М	м	*М*	*м*	m	Э	э	*Э*	*э*	é
Н	н	*Н*	*н*	n	Ю	ю	*Ю*	*ю*	yu
О	о	*О*	*о*	o	Я	я	*Я*	*я*	ya
П	п	*П*	*п*	p					

Before 1918 I i (*I i*) was used instead of И и before vowels and й; also in the word мiръ 'world' to distinguish it from миръ 'peace' and мvръ 'myrrh'; all three are now written мир. Ѣ ѣ (*Ѣ ѣ*) was used mainly on historical grounds in certain words and forms where Е е is now written. Ѳ ѳ (*Ѳ ѳ*) and V v (*V v*) were used in Greek loanwords to represent θ and v/οι; they are now replaced by ф and и. At the end of a word all consonants were followed by either ъ or ь; the former is no longer written, and serves only to mark off prefixes: съ тѣхъ поръ > с тех пор, but съѣсть > съесть.

Note that the substitution of the apostrophe for the hard sign (ъ), occasionally found in Russian texts, is incorrect.

[1] Not treated as a separate letter in Russian, and normally written without the diaeresis; neither of these statements is true of Belorussian.

The extra sorts called for by the other Cyrillic-using languages are: Belorussian ў (= w); Macedonian ѓ (= g′), ѕ (= dz), ј (= j), љ (= lj), њ (= nj), ќ (= k′), and џ (= dž); Serbian Ђ, ђ (= d), ј (= j), љ (= lj), њ (= nj), Ћ, ћ (= ć), and џ (= dž); and Ukrainian є (= ye), and ï (= yi) (ґ = g is now obsolete).

In some Macedonian and Serbian founts cursive г, п, and т are in the form of superior-barred cursive *ī*, *ū*, and *ū* respectively.

Note that, except in certain ancient texts, the term 'Cyrillic' is to be understood of the above characters and not the special fount of that name.

Abbreviations

Modern Russian non-literary texts abound in abbreviations. Details of these are available in D. I. Alekseev's dictionary—*Slovar' sokrashcheniĭ russkogo yazȳka* (Moscow, 1983).

Abbreviations of compound terms formed from their initial letters are set in lower case, with space of line (except when hyphenated), and pointed, e.g. и т. д., и пр., *but* с.-д. Abbreviations by contraction, e.g. д-р, are unpointed.

Abbreviations consisting of capital initial letters, e.g. СССР, are set close without medial or final points. When declined, such abbreviations add flexional endings in closed-up lower case, e.g. ГОСТа.

Abbreviations for metric and other units used in scientific measurement are usually set in cursive and are not followed by a full point; abbreviated qualifying adjectives have the full point, however, e.g. 5 *кв. км*, etc.

Commonly used abbreviations which are pronounced syllabically and declined, e.g. вуз, are not followed by a full point.

Bibliographical lists[1]

The author's name should be followed by his or her initials. Titles of books and articles (in upright) and names of publishing houses are *not* given within guillemets:

Тимирязев К. А. Земледелие и физиология растений. М.-Л.: Книга, 1965.   215 с.

Петрович Г. В. Через ближний космос во вселенную. — Авиация и космонавтика, 1962, № 6, с. 8—12.

Transliterated titles should follow English practice for the use of italic and quotation marks but not of capitals.

Capital and lower case

Capital initial letters are in general less commonly used in Russian than in English.

Use lower-case initials for:

(*a*) Nouns and adjectives formed from personal names, e.g. толстовство, марксизм.

(*b*) Nationalities and names of nationals and of inhabitants of towns, e.g. таджик, Tadzhik; англичанин, Englishman; москвич, Moscovite.

(*c*) Adjectives formed from geographical names, except when they form part of a proper name or the name of an institution, e.g. европейские государства, European states; *but* Челябинский тракторный завод, Chelyabinsk Tractor Works.

(*d*) Non-proper-name elements in the titles of administrative areas of the USSR other than Union or Autonomous Republics, e.g. Курганская область, Kurgan Region; *but* Туркменская Советская Социалистическая Республика, Turkmen Soviet Socialist Republic.

[1] A detailed account of the Russian method of describing titles in bibliographical lists is given in N. A. Nikiforovskaya's *Bibliograficheskoe opisanie* (Leningrad, 1978).

(*e*) Words other than the first in titles of international or non-Soviet organizations and societies: Американская федерация труда, American Federation of Labor; but names of countries take capitals: Соединённые Штаты Америки, United States of America; so too Организация Объединённых Наций, United Nations Organization.

(*f*) Words other than the first in titles of Soviet ministries, administrative organs, and Party and public organizations not of a 'unique' nature, e.g. Государственный комитет Совета Министров СССР по новой технике (note capitals for the 'unique' Совета Министров).

(*g*) Words other than the first in titles of institutions: Академия наук СССР, Academy of Sciences of the USSR; but in titles beginning with an adjective only the noun is lower-case: Государственный Исторический музей, State Historical Museum.

(*h*) Days of the week and names of the months, but note Первое мая and 1-е Мая for the May Day holiday (the capitalization in the latter form is due to the fact that the ordinal number does not count as the 'first word').

(*i*) Titles of literary and musical works, newspapers, and journals, except the first word and proper names: «Отцы и дети»; «Иван Сусанин».

(*j*) Personal names used to indicate character: донжуан, a Don Juan; меценат, a Maecenas.

(*k*) Ranks, titles, etc.: св. Николай, St. Nicholas; кн. Оболенский, Prince Obolenskiĭ; проф. Сидоров, Prof. Sidorov; полковник Иванов, Col. Ivanov.

(*l*) Geographic terms forming part of the name of an area or place: остров Рудольфа, Rudolph Island; Северный полюс, the North Pole.

(*m*) The non-proper-name element in street and similar names: площадь Маяковского, Mayakovskiĭ Square.

(*n*) Names of wars, other than those with titles which refer directly to their character: франко-прусская война, Franco-Prussian War, *but* Великая Отечественная война, Great Patriotic War.

(*o*) Names (other than the first word) of historical events and battles: Кровавое воскресенье, Bloody Sunday; Полтавская битва, the Battle of Poltava.

(*p*) Names (other than the first word) of congresses, agreements, documents, prizes, etc.: Вашингтонское соглашение, the Washington Agreement; Атлантийская хартия, the Atlantic Charter; Ленинская премия, Lenin Prize.

(*q*) The pronoun of the first person singular, я = I (except, of course, when used at the beginning of a sentence). Note that the personal and possessive pronouns of the second person plural (вы and ваш, etc.) take an initial capital when used of individuals in texts addressed to them, e.g. in letters.

The combination of capitals with small capitals is not found in Russian typography.

Dash

Dashes (em rules)[1] are much used in Russian texts, in particular:

(*a*) As a substitute for the copula in nominal statements: Волга — самая большая река в Европе, the Volga is the longest European river.

(*b*) To indicate omission of the verb, e.g. Один рабочий несёт астролябию, другой — треногу, one of the workmen carries the theodolite, the other the tripod.

(*c*) To indicate 'from . . . to . . .': 1946—1950, линия Москва—Горький (the Moscow–Gor'kiĭ line).

---

[1] En rules are not used in Russian typography; em rules close up, as in (*c*), take their place.

(d) Before, and to divide off, statements in dialogue set in paragraphs:

— Я вас люблю, — сказал князь.
— Простите...
— Что простить? — спросил князь Андрей.

Note that when dialogue is set continuously the direct-speech elements are divided off not only by dashes but also by guillemets: Десятник махнул рукой. «Мищенко вчера свой экскаватор утопил», — сказал он мрачно. — «Как? — вскипел Правдин. — Так это же сотни тысяч рублей!» — «Да, конечно!..» — согласился десятник...

Guillemets alone are used to distinguish occasional spoken words, e.g. Она громко закричала: «За мной!»

They are also used if the quoted words are from a letter or soliloquy, though the author's words are none the less divided off by dashes in such cases: «Боже мой, — подумал Мартин, — эта каналья разъезжает в пульмановских вагонах, а я голодаю!..» — Ярость охватила его.

Note in the above examples the use of the comma in addition to the dash to divide off the quoted from the author's words. Where the quoted words end with omission points or an exclamation or question mark, commas are not required. This rule applies whether or not guillemets are present.

Division of words

Russian syllables end in a vowel, and word-division is basically syllabic. However, there are many exceptions to this generalization, most of which are connected with Russian word-formation.

Consonant groups may be taken over entire or divided where convenient (provided at least one

consonant is taken over), subject to the following
rules:

A consonant should not be separated from the
prefix, root, or suffix of which it forms a part,
e.g. род-ной, под-бежать, мещан-ство are correct
divisions.

Divide between double consonants, e.g. класс-
сами, except where this conflicts with the preceding
rule: класс-ный.

The letters ъ, ь, and й should never be separated
from the letter preceding them, e.g. подъ-|езд.

Do not divide between initials; try to avoid
dividing between initials and a surname.

Abbreviated titles, e.g. проф., ул. (before a
street-name), should not be separated from the
name to which they relate.

Letter abbreviations, e.g. РСФСР, ТУ-104,
и т. д., may not be divided.

A single letter or two or more consonants without a vowel may not be either hyphenated at the
end of a line or carried over: к-руглый, ст-рела,
жидко-сть are incorrect.

Hyphens

The hyphen is used:

(a) In nouns consisting of two noun elements,
one of which reinforces or qualifies the sense of the
other, and which are linked without an interpolated vowel: генерал-губернатор, Governor-General,
but кровообращение, circulation of the blood.

(b) In compound place-names, Russian or foreign,
consisting of separable words: Каменец-Подольск,
Ростов-на-Дону, Рио-де-Жанейро, Ла-Плата (exception: Ламанш, the Channel), Сан-Франциско,
Сохо-сквер. If, however, the place-name consists
of a Russian adjective declined as such and a noun,

there are no hyphens: Нижний Новгород, Вышний Волочёк.

(c) In compound points of the compass (nouns and adjectives).

(d) In compound adjectives (i) derived from nouns with complementary meanings, as, for example, журнально-газетный, periodical and newspaper; or (ii) indicating shades of colour: темно-коричневый, dark-brown.

Italic and letter-spacing

Italic (*kursiv*; cursive) and letter-spacing (*razryadka*) are used to distinguish or emphasize a word or words in the text. Of the two methods, letter-spacing is perhaps the more commonly employed for this purpose, though words cited in linguistic texts are always given in cursive. Guillemets are used to show that a word is being used in an unfamiliar or special sense.

Titles of books and journals should be printed in upright type and not in cursive (see *Bibliographical lists* above).

Numerals, dates, reference figures, fractions

Numbers from 10,000 upwards are divided off into thousands by 3-unit spaces, and not by commas, e.g. 26 453; below 10,000 they are set close, e.g. 9999.

The decimal comma is used in place of the decimal point, e.g. 0,36578.

Ordinal numbers are followed by a contracted adjectival termination except when they are used in dates: 5-й год *but* 7 ноября 1917 г.

Superior footnote-reference figures in the text precede punctuation marks and are followed by a 3-unit space, e.g. ...ero[1] . In the footnote itself the reference figure or symbol is a superior and is followed by a space but no point.

The form of fraction with an oblique divider (solidus) is preferred, e.g. $^1/_5$ (except in mathematical work).

Inclusive dates are not abbreviated, e.g. 1946—1950. A financial or academic year which covers parts of two calendar years is expressed thus: 1946/47.

Plays

In dialogue the names of the speakers usually precede the words spoken and are either letter-spaced or, less often, set in bold. They are also found centred. Stage directions, if set immediately after the name of the speaker or within the body, or at the end, of the spoken words, are set in cursive within parentheses:

Лопахин. Пришёл поезд, слава Богу. Который час?

Дуняша. Скоро два. (*Тушит свечу.*) Уже светло.

General stage directions are set centrally (or full left and with their last line centred) in upright but smaller type.

Punctuation

The chief points of difference between the Russian and the English punctuation systems relate to the use of the comma, omission points, and dashes. For the last see *Dash*; for guillemets see also *Dash*, *Italic and letter-spacing*, and *Quotation marks*; for punctuation of abbreviations see *Abbreviations*.

The comma is used more often than in English, and always:

(*a*) Before subordinate clauses introduced by

interrogative-relative pronouns and adverbs, participles, and gerunds.

(*b*) To divide off co-ordinate clauses joined by conjunctions such as и, да, а, но, или.

(*c*) Between a principal clause and a subordinate clause introduced by a conjunction. Note that when the conjunction что forms the second element of a compound conjunction, the comma precedes the first part unless it is desired to stress the close causal or temporal connection between the two parts of the sentence:

Люди умирали, потому что была эпидемия.

People were dying, for there was an epidemic.

Люди умирали потому, что была эпидемия.

There was an epidemic, so people were dying.

In substantival and adjectival enumerations in which there is a single, final и, it is not preceded by a comma.

For the use of the comma in conjunction with the dash see *Dash* (last paragraph).

The three dots indicating an interruption (omission points) are in one piece. They are always spaced at their open end (except when guillemets precede or follow), and set close at their engaged end, e.g. Это... я... умираю; ...уже; *but* «...мы должны отвергнуть». When omission points coincide with an exclamation or question mark, they form one piece with it and are reduced to two points: !.., ?..

Omission points are never immediately followed by a full point.

Where omission points (or an exclamation or question mark) precede quotation marks, the latter are never followed by a full point, e.g. «За мной!»

Quotation marks

Two forms of quotation mark are used in Russian: (i) opening double commas on the line followed by closing superior turned double commas (*lapochki*), and (ii) (double) guillemets (*ëlochki*). Of the two, guillemets are by far the more common form but in the remarks which follow the word will be taken to cover both forms of quotation mark.

Apart from their use to indicate direct speech and soliloquy (see *Dash* (*d*)), guillemets are used (*a*) to show that a word or words are being employed in a special sense, and (*b*) with titles of literary works, journals, and pictures, and with names of ships, factories, and organizations (except when the latter consist of initials or conventional abbreviations), e.g. роман «Война и мир», журнал «Новый мир», картина Репина «Не ждали», завод «Серп и молот», издательство «Книга», *but* Госиздат, ГЭС.

Quotation marks are not duplicated unless they are of differing design, e.g. Он ответил: «Я приехал вчера на пароходе «Казань» (note the final guillemet which covers both the end of the name of the ship and the end of the sentence); *but* Он ответил: „Я приехал вчера на пароходе «Казань»".

For punctuation after quotation marks see *Dash* and *Punctuation*.

Spacing

The dash (except between numerals and when linking extremities, when it is set close) is 3-unit-spaced at either end; all other punctuation marks are set close.

For spacing of omission points see *Punctuation* (last three paragraphs).

Transliteration

The British Standard scheme given in the Table on p. 120 has much to commend it. It may be used with or without diacritics, though in the latter case it loses the advantage of reversibility. If desired, -y may be used to express final -й, -ий, and -ый in proper names, e.g. Tolstoy, Dostoevsky, Grozny. Another commonly used British system agrees with the British Standard scheme with the following exceptions: е = *ye* initially and after ъ, ь, or a vowel; ё = *yo* (*o* after ж, ч, ш, or щ); й = *y*; final -ий, -ый = *y* in proper names or titles.

For philological work the International System (ISO/R9 = Table C in British Standard 2979: 1958) is recommended.

A comparative table covering seven transliteration systems is printed on p. 65 of R. Neiswender's *Guide to Russian Reference and Language Aids* (New York, 1962).

SPANISH

Accent

ACCENT in Spanish does not indicate vowel quality, nor musical pitch, but stress. This is indicated by the acute (´) accent. The only other diacritical marks used are the tilde on the ñ, which is a separate letter in the alphabet, and the diaeresis on *ü*, which is used after *g* before *e* or *i* when *u* forms a diphthong with *e* or *i* and is not merely used to indicate hard *g* before *e* or *i*. (See under *Orthography*.) Accents should be set on capitals, but some authors prefer to omit the acute.

There are two kinds of stress, the *normal* and the *abnormal*. The normal stress is never indicated by an accent; the abnormal stress is always indicated by the acute.

The normal stress occurs:

(1) In words ending in a vowel or *n* or *s*, on the last syllable but one: termino ('I terminate') but terminó ('he terminated'), término ('term'); intereses plural of interés. The suffix *-ción* (equivalent of English *-tion*) makes in the plural *-ciones*.

(2) In words ending in a consonant other than *n* or *s*, on the last syllable: ciudad, reloj, Jerez, Ortiz, but Cádiz, Velázquez (and so other surnames in -ez, e.g. González).

When *a*, *e*, or *o* stands immediately before or after *i* or *u* they form a diphthong, as do *iu* and *ui*: in a stressed syllable the *a*, *e*, or *o* will be stressed, or the second vowel in *iu*, *ui*. Thus aire, dioses, ruido, and in an unstressed syllable academia. Exceptions are marked with the accent: armonía, hebraísta, flúido, vivió. An intervening *h* is ignored: rehúso, cf. transeúnte.

When object-pronouns are attached to a verb, the stress rules apply to the group as a whole: traiga but tráiganoslas. However, an accent already present in the verb is retained, acabóse (but el acabose as a noun).

Infinitives in aír, eír, and oír should now be written with the accent, the preterites dio, fue, fui, vio without.

The words a ('to'), e ('and'), o, u ('or') are now printed without accents, except that between arabic numerals o is written ó: 2 ó 3, but II o III, 7 u 8.

The words cuál, cómo, cuándo, cuánto, dónde, pórque, qué, and quién take the acute when used as interrogatives or exclamations; otherwise no accent is required.

Accent differentiates the meaning of the following: dé ('may give', de 'of'), él ('he', el 'the'), más ('more', mas 'but'), mí ('me', mi 'my'), sí ('self', 'yes', si 'if'), *sólo* ('only', *solo* 'alone'), *aún* ('still', of time, *aun* 'even').

Alphabet

The groups *ch* and *ll* are treated as compound letters, coming after *c* and *l*; *ñ* comes after *n*.

Dash

The em rule indicating parenthetic matter is set close up on the words it introduces or closes, and with a line space between it and the body of the sentence: la pronunciación figurada —cuyo uso es internacional— debe ser . . .

Division of words

A consonant between two vowels and the second of two consonants must be taken over to the next line. But note carefully the following rules.

ch, *ll*, and *rr* are indivisible because they represent single sounds, and must be taken over: mu-chacho, arti-llería, pe-rro. *n* with tilde (*ñ* = *gn* in 'cognac') must be treated as a single consonant and therefore taken over in division: ca-ñón.

Consonants, except *s*, followed by *l* or *r* must be taken over with *l* or *r* undivided, but an exception is *tl* after initial *a*. Examples: ha-blar, a-flictivo, a-planar, a-prender, a-trio; but is-lámico, Is-raelítico, At-lántico.

Exactly contrary to the Latin rule, *s-t*, *s-p* must be divided: Es-teban, es-trella; ins-tar, ins-piración.

Divide compounds into their component parts, except where they contain *s*+consonant or *rr*: des-hacer, sub-lunar, but circuns-tancia, co-rregir, inte-rrumpir. Diphthongs must never be divided.

Orthography

Note especially the common use of the single consonants *s*, *l*, *n*, *c* in such words as: disipa, óseo, ilegal, inocente, ocultar, necesario. But print *nn* in innovación, innumerable, and *cc* in acceso, acción. Note also the dissimilation of *nm* in conmemoración, inmediatamente, inmenso, inmortal, etc. Print: aceptación, acomodación, asimilación, subrogar, sugestión, sujeto, suplicio.

Hard *g* before *e* or *i* is indicated by the insertion of *u*: guerrilla, guitarra.

Punctuation

Punctuation marks are similar to those used in English, but note that the exclamation (!) and the question (?) marks are inserted both before (inverted) and after the word or phrase, e.g. ¡Ve! ¿Dónde?

Quotation marks

Quotations are indicated by guillemets, dialogue by em rules (set close up); but when an author prefers the English style, his instructions are to be followed, and the compositor should be guided by the directions given with the work.

CATALAN AND PORTUGUESE

THESE languages have much in common with Spanish, but from the typographical point of view there are important differences. To note in both:

The character *ç*.

Digraphs and accented letters are not separated in the alphabetical order.

The group *rr* is divided.

Inverted question and exclamation marks are not used

Words ending in *i* + vowel or *u* + vowel are in the absence of a written accent stressed on the *i* or *u*. Thus Catalan acadèmia indicates the same incidence of stress as Spanish academia, but Portuguese academia a different one.

CATALAN

Note the group *l·l*, different from *ll*. At the end of a line *l·l* is divided *l-l*, *ll* and *ny* taken over.

Accents on vowels may indicate stress or vowel quality: they are ´ (on *e, i, o, u*), ` (on *a, e, o*), and ¨ (on *i* and *u*).

PORTUGUESE

Take over *ch, lh, nh*. When a word is divided at a pre-existing hyphen, repeat the hyphen at the beginning of the next line. This is especially frequent with object pronouns: thus dar-lho is divided dar-|-lho.

The accents used in Portuguese are ´ ` ^ ~ (til) ¨; since 1945, however, ¨ has been used only in Brazil; since 1972 ` in Portugal has been confined to the fused forms à (às), àquele (etc.) for a a, a aquele. In general, Brazil uses accents discarded in Portugal but also reflects differences in pronunciation: to Portuguese rapidamente, linguístico, ele, falámos, elénico, António correspond Brazilian ràpidamente, lingüístico, êle (all previously in use in Portugal), falamos, elênico, Antônio (all indicating divergence of pronunciation). Brazilian spelling also simplifies various consonant groups: ação, ato, dicionário for acção, acto, diccionário.

TURKISH

NOTE the accented letters *Ç ç Ş ş* (with cedilla) *Ğ ğ* (with *round* accent). *I ı* and *İ i* are separate letters; *î* or *ī* in copy should be set as *ı*, but *â î û* set thus. Do not use the ligature *fi*, but set *fı* or *fi* as the case may be.

WELSH

THE Welsh alphabet consists of 28 letters: *a b c ch d dd e f ff g ng h i l ll m n o p ph r rh s t th u w y; j* is used in borrowed words, *k* and *v* are very frequent in medieval texts but now obsolete.

Note especially:

(1) the separate ranking of the digraphs *ch dd ff ng ll ph rh th* (but NB not *ngh mh nh nn rr*);

(2) the position of *ng* (which, however, is occasionally two letters, see below on word-division—in that case ranking between *nff* and *nh*);

(3) *rh* counts as a separate letter at the start of a word or syllable only, i.e. after a consonant but not a vowel: *route* comes before *rhad* 'cheap', *cynrychioli* 'to represent' before *cynrhon* 'maggots', but *arholi* 'to examine' before *arian* 'money';

(4) *w* is usually, *y* always, a vowel.

All vowels may take a circumflex; usage is not entirely consistent, but some pairs of words are distinguished only by the accent: *dy dŷ* 'your [familiar singular] house', *bûm* 'I was' or *bum* 'five' in *Atebwch bum cwestiwn* 'Answer five questions'. There are four different words *a* besides the name of the letter, and three *â*. Acute, grave, and diaeresis are also found: most frequent is *á* in final syllables (e.g. *casáu* 'to hate') and *ï* before a vowel (*copïo* 'to copy'); the letter with the diaeresis always precedes or follows another vowel.

A word consisting of an apostrophe followed by a single letter must be set close up with the preceding word: *cerddai'r bachgen a'i fam i'ch pentref*, 'the boy and his mother used to walk to your village'.

Division of words

Single letters, including the digraphs *ch, dd, ff, ll, ph, th* must not be divided: *ng* is indivisible when

a single letter, but not when it represents $n+g$:
this happens most frequently in the verb *dangos*
'to show' and its derivatives, compounds ending in
-garwch or *-garwr* (e.g. *ariangarwr* 'money-lover'),
place-names beginning with *Llan-* (e.g. *Llangefni*),
and in *Bangor*. Thus *cyng-aneddol* but *a ddan-
goswyd*.

Diphthongs and triphthongs must not be divided:
they are *ae, ai, au, aw, ayw, ei, eu, ew, ey, iw, oe, oi,
ou, ow, oyw, wy, yw* (in earlier texts also *ay, oy*), and
other combinations beginning with *i* and *w*, in which
these letters are consonants. The presence of a
circumflex or an acute does not affect word-division,
but it is legitimate to divide after a vowel bearing
the diaeresis, as also after a diphthong or triphthong
before another vowel. Thus *barddonï-aidd* 'bardic',
gloyw-ach 'brighter', *ieu-anc* 'young'.

A suffix beginning with $i+$vowel must be broken
off: *casgl-iad* 'collection'; here the *i* counts as a
consonant; so too with $w+$vowel (but *an-nwyl, eg-
lwys*, and a few other words in which *-wy-* is not a
suffix and the *w* is vocalic).

Otherwise the rule is to follow etymology rather
than pronunciation. As a rough guide: take back
a single consonant other than *h* except after a prefix
(especially *di-, go-, tra-*), *g-l* but *s-gl* (and so similar
groups), but suffixes should be broken off; take
back in doubtful cases when a specialist cannot be
consulted. Particularly in narrow measure, two-
letter suffixes may have to be taken over, above all
the plural *-au*. However, it is always safe to divide
l-rh, ng-h, m-h, n-h (but *n-nh*), *n-n, n-rh, r-r*, and
after a vowel *r-h*. NB. Initial *gwl-, gwn-, gwr-*, and
their mutated forms must not be divided, since the
w is consonantal; *gwlad* 'country', *(hen) wlad* '(old)
country'; *gwneud* 'to do', *(ei) wneud* 'to do (it)';
gwraig 'woman', *(y) wraig* '(the) woman', cannot be
divided.

Mutations and other changes

Initial consonants, in certain grammatical contexts, are replaced by others in a process called mutation: *cath* 'cat' but *fy nghath* 'my cat', *ei gath* 'his cat', *ei chath* 'her cat'; *Brymbo, Caerdydd* (Cardiff), *Dinbych* (Denbigh), *Gwent, Penybont-ar-Ogwr* (Bridgend), *Tonypandy* give *i Frymbo* 'to Brymbo' (and *o Frymbo* 'from Brymbo'), *ym Mrymbo* 'in Brymbo'; *i Gaerdydd, yng Nghaerdydd; i Ddinbych, yn Ninbych, i Went, yng Ngwent, i Benybont-ar-Ogwr, ym Mhenybont-ar-Ogwr; i Donypandy, yn Nhonypandy*. Oxford is *Rhydychen* (*rhyd* 'ford', *ychen* 'oxen'), but 'from Oxford' is *o Rydychen*; University is *Prifysgol*, but 'Printer to the University' is *Argraffwr i'r Brifysgol*. The full range of mutations is *b* to *f* or *m*; *c* to *ch, g,* or *ngh*; *d* to *dd* or *n*; *g* omitted or to *ng*; *ll* to *l*; *m* to *f*; *p* to *b, mh,* or *ph*; *rh* to *r*; *t* to *d, nh,* or *th*. NB. The abbreviations of mutated words are not exempt: where *llinell* 'line' and *llinellau* 'lines' are mutated to *linell* or *linellau*, there *ll.* and *llau.* are mutated to *l.* and *lau.* Thus *l.* and *ll.* are both singular.

Initial vowels may acquire a preliminary *h* (*offer* 'tools', *ein hoffer* 'our tools') and changes of stress within a word may cause *h* to appear or disappear and double *n* or *r* to be simplified: *brenin* 'king', *brenhinoedd* 'kings'; *brenhines* 'queen', *breninesau* 'queens'; *corrach* 'dwarf', *corachod* 'dwarfs'; *cynneddf* 'faculty', *cyneddfau* 'faculties'; *cynnin* 'shred', *cynhinion* 'shreds'; *dihareb* 'proverb', *diarhebion* 'proverbs'.

But in medieval Welsh we find *brenhin* for 'king', and *breninoedd* was misguidedly written (though not pronounced) in the nineteenth century.

Punctuation

Punctuation and other conventions are as in English with the exception of word-division.

BIBLIOGRAPHY

THIS list is not exhaustive, but is a selection designed to provide a fairly comprehensive and reliable guide. Not all the authorities cited in this book are given again here. A bibliography for scientific work will be found on p. 60.

The Oxford Spelling Dictionary (Oxford, 1986)

The Oxford Dictionary for Writers and Editors (Oxford, 1981)

British Printing Industries Federation and Publishers Association, *Book Production Practice* (1978)

J. Butcher, *Copy-editing*, second edition (Cambridge, 1981)

J. Butcher, *Typescripts, Proofs and Indexes* (Cambridge, 1980)

H. W. Fowler, *Modern English Usage*, second edition (Oxford, 1965)

S. Jennett, *The Making of Books*, fifth edition (London, 1974)

University of Chicago Press, *A Manual of Style*, thirteenth edition (Chicago, 1982)

University of Chicago Press, *The Chicago Guide to the Preparing of Electronic Manuscripts* (Chicago, 1987)

H. Williamson, *Methods of Book Design*, third edition (1983)

British Standards Institution:
Alphabetical Arrangement. BS 1749 (1969)
Bibliographical References. BS 1629, second edition (1976)
Citing Publications. BS 5605 (1978)
Copy Preparation and Proof Correction. BS 5261 (1975-6), Parts 1-2

Letter Symbols, Signs and Abbreviations. BS
     1991 (1961–   )
Transliteration of Cyrillic and Greek Characters.
     BS 2979 (1958)
Type-face Nomenclature. BS 2961 (1967)

APPENDIX

RULES FOR COMPOSITION
AND MAKE-UP[1]

THESE rules are for normal bookwork: they are to be followed wherever practicable. Exceptions can be made for narrow measures and when the rearrangement of type to conform with these rules would prove unreasonable. In borderline cases supervisors are to be consulted for a decision whether an exception is to be made.

DIVISION OF WORDS

Avoid divisions if at all possible, having regard for the requirements of good typography. Where word-breaks are necessary, however, the following rules apply:

(*a*) A minimum of two characters may be left behind and a minimum of three characters carried over at a word-break.

(*b*) Two successive hyphens only are allowed at the ends of lines.

(*c*) A divided word should not end a right-hand page.

(*d*) If a right-hand page is a full-page illustration or table, the facing left-hand page should not end with a hyphen.

---

[1] Definitions for spacing terms given on p. xi apply also to the appendix.

FOOTNOTES

(*a*) A footnote should start on the same page as the text reference, but may overrun on to subsequent pages. If this is necessary, the footnote reference should occur, if possible, in the last line of text of the page in which the footnote starts. In the page(s) on which the note is continued there should be at least three lines of text. The overrun footnote will appear immediately below the text of the following page(s) and be separated from further footnotes by a space, not a rule (a line space when footnotes are in double column). If other notes are turned over, insert a catchline at the foot of the first page, placed full right in the line of white at the foot (i.e. extra to normal page depth): [*See opposite page/p.   for n.   cont. and n(n).*   ].

Similarly if the overrun of a footnote jumps one or more pages for any reason (plates, etc.), insert a catchline: [*cont. on p.*   ].

An incomplete footnote should not end a page with a full point (i.e. it should be seen to be un-finished).

(*b*) One single-line note on a page should be centred; two or more single-line notes on a page should be ranged on the left, the whole being centred on the longest.

(*c*) A short note may be set complete in the break-line of another note provided it is set full right, preferably with more than three ems between the notes.

(*d*) Short notes may be run on in the same line with preferably at least 3 ems between them, the line being centred. Where there are several short footnotes, they should be ranged in columns with a minimum of a 3-em space between the longest lines in the columns.

(*e*) Footnotes with identical wording should be set once only on any one page and the footnote references re-numbered accordingly. This will not apply if numbering runs through a chapter or section.

(*f*) Where apparatus criticus occurs as well as footnotes, it is to appear, with the first line indented one em, above the footnotes, and separated from them by a short thin rule, full left. However, if there are, in addition, *original* footnotes, they should appear above app. crit. and editorial notes, separated by a short thin rule, full left.

(*g*) Where a single short note occurs below app. crit. it is to be set 1 em from the left and not centred (see (*b*) above).

(*h*) Where footnotes are to be set in two columns, a footnote of one, two, or three (single-column) lines appearing on its own on one page is to be rearranged as full measure and centred. Similarly, two footnotes, one of two lines and one of one line, should be treated in like manner.

(*i*) With double-column footnotes a break-line at the top of the second column is to be avoided where possible.

(*j*) Footnotes should be numbered from 1 on each page, unless there is a special direction to number continuously through chapters or sections.

(*k*) Footnote references should be placed outside punctuation, but inside the closing parenthesis when referring to matter within the parentheses.

(*l*) Footnotes should begin with the numbers indented 1 em, but where numbers change to tens or hundreds, numbers should range on the inside for that page only (i.e. the room for the additional figure will come out of the em space).

See TABLES (*h*) for style of footnotes to tables.

GENERAL

(*a*) No more than two successive lines should begin or end with the same word.

(*b*) Rectos have odd numbers, versos even.

(*c*) Leading between paragraphs is not allowed in continuous text.

(*d*) A right-hand page should not end with a colon which is introducing poetry, examples, etc.

(*e*) Marginal notes are to be set on the outside edge of the page and, unless otherwise directed, lines should range on the inside against the text.

(*f*) Where lines of text are numbered, the numbers (ranged on the inside) are to appear on the outside margin in prose works but full right in the measure for poetry (but see PLAYS (*h*)).

When marginal notes *and* line numbers occur, the marginal notes should appear on the outer edge of the page and line numbers on the inner edge. Where a folio number (or some other marginal) clashes with a line number in the same margin, the next line should be numbered instead; if this is not possible, the nearest line to the original numbering should be numbered.

(*g*) Pages are all to be of the same depth, but in books of verse pages may be left short, rather than be excessively spaced out. Complete pages of a body size different from the text (e.g. appendices and extracts) should be made up, to the nearest line, to the depth of the text page.

(*h*) Interline spacing must be uniform in normal texts.

(*i*) If possible, avoid a, I, l., ll., pl., p., pp., at the ends of lines; in app. crit. do not end a line with a line number.

(*j*) A minimum of five characters (excluding the full point) is allowed on the last line of a paragraph. Measures greater than 28 ems should have more than five characters.

(*k*) A page or column should not start with the last line of a paragraph even when the line is a full one.

(*l*) A paragraph may start as the last line of a page or column.

(*m*) Unless instructions are given to the contrary, capitals, small capitals, numerals, and punctuation in displayed lines should be letter-spaced.

(*n*) Use lining (ranging) figures for dates, etc., where these occur in lines of capitals, and non-lining figures with lines of even small capitals.

(*o*) In centred displayed headings (chapter titles, crossheads, etc.) keep word spaces even and avoid dividing words. Lines should not be forced out to full measure and *each* line should be centred. Where it is possible, and sensible, avoid having a short single word as the last line.

ILLUSTRATIONS

In this section an illustration should be understood to mean a block plus its underline, if any.

(*a*) As far as possible an illustration and the reference to it should be kept within a two-page opening, with the illustration occurring after the reference. Where the text reads into the illustration the illustration may not be moved unless the text is reworded.

(*b*) Illustrations of approximately half a page or less in depth should be placed slightly above centre with text above and below. (See fig. 1.[1])

[1] All figures are grouped together at the end.

(*c*) Illustrations much greater than half a page in depth can be placed at head or foot of page (preferably the head) to avoid breaking the text into only a few lines above and below the illustration (see fig. 2). The minimum number of lines of text permitted on such pages is five.

(*d*) Where two full-width illustrations are to occur within a two-page opening, one illustration is to appear on each page, positioned as for (*b*) or (*c*) above. However, if the depth of the illustrations allows, they may be set together on one page with at least a line of white between. (See fig. 3.)

(*e*) Where three full-width illustrations are to occur within a two-page opening, two may be set one above the other on one page with text at the foot of the page (a minimum of four lines) and at least a line of white between the two illustrations.

(*f*) Illustrations less than half a page in width should be placed as for (*b*) and (*c*) above, and on the outer edge of the page with the text run round on the inside of the illustration. Underlines should be set to the width of the illustration. (See fig. 4.)

(*g*) To avoid running text round a narrow illustration, the underlines, if of suitable length, can be placed on the inner side of the block (ranging at head for blocks in the upper half of a page, or at foot for blocks in the lower half of a page, and generally with unjustified lines). (See fig. 5.)

(*h*) An illustration greater than half a page but less than a full page in width should be centred with the underline set to the width of the illustration if it makes two or more lines, or centred below the block if it is a single line no wider than the illustration. (See fig. 1.)

(*i*) Illustrations greater than text measure in width will generally be positioned by the Layout department, but if no instructions are given, the illustrations should be centred and the underlines set to text measure.

(*j*) For inset blocks one line of apparent white (including flange on block), equal to the point size of the surrounding type, is to be left at the head and side of the block and one and a half lines below (where other leading can be adjusted to suit this), or one line of apparent white below if necessary for make-up.

(*k*) Between six and nine points white should be left between the underline and the lowest part of the block's printing area, and approximately twelve points between underline and following text.

(*l*) Where two illustrations, each of less than half a page in width, occur on a page they are to be placed side by side. (See fig. 6.)

(*m*) Where two blocks of not too dissimilar depth appear side by side on a page, the bases and/or underlines of the blocks are to range. (See figs. 7–8.)

(*n*) In bookwork, running heads and folios should generally be omitted from full-page illustrations. However, where two or more full-page illustrations occur together and facing pages do not contain a folio, the folio may be centred in parentheses at the top of the page (or at the bottom in books where the folio normally occurs at the foot of pages). This will apply whether the illustrations are turned sideways or not. In journals, headlines should be inserted over full-page illustrations unless the block includes the space of the headline.

(*o*) Illustrations which have to be turned sideways should always be placed with the head of the illustration on the left, whether on left- or right-hand pages.

(*p*) For multi-column make-up the order of illustrations is to be maintained wherever possible.

(*q*) When an underline makes only two or three lines avoid wide word-spacing, word-divisions, and awkward final turns by slight adjustment to the measure of the underline (usually within the width of the block).

MACHINE-READABLE CODES

At present, the adoption of machine-readable codes on books published within the UK is voluntary, therefore not all titles will be affected. When a publisher does opt to print such a code on one of his titles, all the technical and other details are covered by a Specification and Operating Manual on Machine Readable Codes for the Book Trade, published by the Publishers Association, 19 Bedford Square, London WC1B 3HJ. In so far as this specification touches on the work of compositors and readers, the rules may be summarized:

(*a*) Inside the book, the ISBN on the verso of the title-page should be made machine-readable by creating this number as a single, separate line of OCR–A characters which is then imposed:

6 mm clear on all sides from any other print on the title verso;

clear of any print on the title-page itself to avoid any effects from 'show through';

at least 10 mm from the gutter or trimmed edge of the page.

Any further detail may be found in Section 15 of the Specification and Manual.

(*b*) Outside the book, the ISBN is made machine readable by the application of a combined

OCR–A and EAN Bar Code symbol, normally supplied by the publisher as a single piece of film. It is recommended that this symbol appears on the bottom, right-hand corner of the back of the cover or dust jacket. The ISBN should be readable by eye and the bars of the EAN Code kept vertical. The bottom right-hand corner mark of the symbol should be 6 mm clear of the bottom edge and spine of the book. Any further detail may be found in Section 14 of the Specification and Manual.

It is not incumbent on the printer to test the readability or correctness of these symbols; compositors and readers need concern themselves only with the proper placing of the material given to them by the publisher.

NEW CHAPTERS OR SECTIONS

(*a*) When chapters start on fresh pages, the minimum number of lines left on the final page of the previous chapter should be five. (Books with a small format may exceptionally go down to a minimum of three lines.)

(*b*) When page numbers are specifically requested on the first page of a new chapter, they should be placed centrally in the headline in parentheses, letter-spaced. This will not apply, of course, to books having page numbers at the foot.

(*c*) Running heads are not used where a section begins a page and the heading is also the running head. The folio should be placed in parentheses, letter-spaced, and centred. In books where folios occur at the foot of pages, the headline is to be left blank.

(*d*) As a general rule the first paragraph of a chapter or section is to be set full out. Succeeding paragraphs are to be indented 1 em.

(*e*) For books in which chapters/sections run on:

(i) Where the heading is in the same point size as the text, and there is no drop initial, there should be a minimum of two lines of the first paragraph of the new chapter or section at the foot of the page.

(ii) Where the heading is in a point size larger than that of the text, and there is no drop initial, at least three lines should come at the foot of the page.

(iii) With drop initials there must be at least one full line at the end of a page below the initial. (See also THREE-LINE DROP INITIALS.)

(iv) Where there is a line of white towards the foot of a page this must be followed by at least two lines of type.

(v) Where sections are separated by a line of white and the last line of a section falls as the last line of a page, then the new section will start at the head of the next page, the line of white being omitted.

(vi) Where a centred section heading (crosshead) begins a page and a running head also appears on the page there should be a minimum of one line of white between the running head and the section heading.

(vii) Where a new section starts within a page the running head should refer to the first matter appearing on a verso page, and the last matter appearing on a recto page.

PLAYS

Books of plays vary considerably in style, and instructions must be followed for style of speakers' names, indentations, etc.

(*a*) Plays should begin on right-hand pages; acts on

new pages, left or right; scenes run on. Sometimes the title and list of characters will appear together on the right-hand page, and sometimes the characters will be on the verso of the title, facing the text. Follow instructions.

(*b*) Characters' names in entrances, stage directions, and exits should be set distinctively, usually in roman even small capitals (letter-spaced).

(*c*) *Entrances*: capital and lower-case italic centred.

(*d*) *Stage directions*: capital and lower-case italic in square brackets as in the following examples:

(1) JOHN [*eagerly*]. Do come, by all means.

(2) JAMES. Most unpleasant! [*Thunderclap*] Hm! Now we're in for it.

The direction should be set full right preceded by one square bracket in this example:

(3) JOHN. Step aside with me, my love.
      Thou shalt hear my secret wish.
                              [*Leads her to the right*
    MARY. Master, wilt thou trifle yet?
      Can I believe thou'rt in earnest?

(*e*) *Exits*: capital and lower-case italic full right with one square bracket:

    CHARLES. It is well, my friend. Farewell!   [*Exit*

(*f*) Instructions will usually be given for style and arrangement of speakers' names and indentations. Where no other instructions exist, set names in even small capitals, letter-spaced, full left, run into first line of dialogue for verse plays, with remainder of dialogue indented 1 em and turnovers 2 ems. In prose plays, set characters' names full out (as above) with turnovers indented 1 em.

(*g*) *Headlines* should include act and scene numbers, usually across the inner shoulders.

(*h*) *Line numbers* (in fives: rules as for poetry) should appear on the right-hand edge within the text measure if verse, outside if prose.

Care must be observed in numbering lines of plays in verse. Frequently a line is made up of the speeches of more than one character. Such parts of a line must be set with the second part a space of the line clear to the right of the first part and the third part a space of the line clear to the right of the second part. If the second (or third) part is too long to allow this, the part should be set full right and allowed to run back under the first (or second) part as necessary: turn-overs to these parts must be avoided.

Example:

CAM. Business, my lord! I think most understand		(1)
Bohemia stays here longer.		
LEON. Ha!		(2)
CAM. Stays here longer.		
LEON. Ay, but why?		(3)
CAM. To satisfy your highness and the entreaties		(4)
Of our most gracious mistress.		
LEON. Satisfy!		(5)
The entreaties of your mistress! satisfy!		(6)

(*i*) *Mixture of prose and verse*. Where isolated verse (e.g. a song) occurs in a prose play it should be centred, following the rules for poetry.

Where prose and verse alternate in a play (e.g. *Twelfth Night*), the verse and its speakers' names should be indented or full out in the same style as the prose.

POETRY

(*a*) The standard space of the line will be the thick space. If turnover lines compel a variation from the standard, the general rules for spacing should be applied (see SPACING (*a*)).

(*b*) Whenever a poetic quotation is given a line (or more) to itself, it is not to be placed within quotation marks (unless the quotation marks are included in the quotation); therefore any quotation within it should be in single quotes, not double for a quote within a quote. However, when a line of poetry runs on with the (prose) text, then quotation marks are to be used.

(*c*) In general, poetry (including blank verse) should be centred on the longest line on each page, unless such line is disproportionately long, when the matter should be centred optically. This can be achieved by striking an average of the longest lines. The aim must be to secure a balance of 'white' on a page.

(*d*) In a book of poems each poem should be centred individually, page by page.

(*e*) Where prose text matter is broken up by poetic quotations and more than one quotation appears on a page, each quotation should be dealt with separately unless there are successive extracts from the same poem, when it is usually desirable to have a common indentation (rule (*c*) above will then apply).

(*f*) Copy should be followed for capitals at the beginnings of lines (modern verse sometimes has none). In Greek and Latin verse it is usual to capitalize only the first word of each paragraph.

(*g*) Turnovers in general should be indented 1 em more than the greatest indentation of the poem, but must be adjusted to suit the metre of the verse where necessary.

(*h*) When poetry has to run on to another page the splitting of short stanzas (i.e. carrying part of a stanza on to the next page) should be avoided whenever possible. Two paired lines (e.g. consecutive rhyming lines) should not be separated.

(*i*) To indicate the omission of a line (or more) a 'line' of medial points, separated by 2-em spaces, should be inserted. The first and last points should fall 2 ems inside the measure of the longest line.

(*j*) Sources at the end of verse should range on the right with the longest line of the poem on the page on which the source appears. If the source is too long to get into a single line within the width of the longest line, it should start approximately 1 em further in than the deepest indentation of the poem and turn over as required, turnovers being ranged on the left with the beginning of the source. The first line of the source should be normal-spaced and ranged on the right with the longest line of the poem (as above).

Examples:

> (1) The day is done, and the darkness
> Falls from the wings of Night,
> As a feather is wafted downward
> From an eagle in his flight.
>
> (Longfellow)

> (2) Come, old friend, sit down and listen!
> As it passes thus between us,
> How its wavelets laugh and glisten
> In the head of old Silenus!
>
> (From 'Drinking Song', a ballad
> by Longfellow)

(*k*) Where lines of poetry are numbered (e.g. in fives) the numbers are to appear on the right-hand edge within the text measure. If a line is too long to allow the number to be inserted, then the next line or, if that is too long, the preceding line should be numbered instead.

(*l*) Where a poem has varying indentation the copy must be followed. Generally, a line will range on the left with the line(s) with which it rhymes.

SPACING

(*a*) Close and even spacing is the usual standard. This means aiming for a middle space or less. The minimum should be a thin space, with a little less in exceptional cases and for narrow-set and close-fitting founts. Ideally the maximum should be an en space. Display lines set in one of the Chancery italic founts (Arrighi, Bembo, Blado) should always be very close spaced (thin or less).

(*b*) The space of the line should be used after all points in normal text. A special direction, 'Close, with extra space after sentence full points', will be given for works which require an extra space after sentence full points (e.g. some bibliographies, dictionaries, and Classical texts).

(*c*) Letter-spacing within words is not allowed for overcoming justification problems (except very occasionally, e.g. in extremely narrow measures).

(*d*) Where an em rule or a hyphen occurs in a line of letter-spaced capitals, small capitals, or figures, there should be a corresponding space each side of the rule or hyphen.

(*e*) Where suitable, bad spacing and word-divisions may be avoided in lists (contents, etc.) and in some column and tabular matter by leaving lines un-justified on the right.

TABLES

(*a*) Where the text does not read into the table: these tables should appear as near to the point of reference as possible—preferably following it—and be positioned as for illustrations. (See ILLUSTRATIONS (*b-e*).)

(*b*) Where the text reads into the table: these tables (usually open, unnumbered, and introduced by a colon) may not be moved unless the text is reworded.

(*c*) Vertical rules should be omitted and horizontal rules kept to a minimum, although head and tail rules should be included in most cases. In particular, tables having only two columns should be set without rules. Head and tail rules (R4) are to be heavier than internal rules (R2).

(*d*) When (ruled) tables are open at the sides, the horizontal rules should not extend beyond the width of the first and last columns.

(*e*) Column headings (usually set in roman capitals and lower case) should range on the left, with the lines unjustified, and, unless unsuitable, be set full left in the column. The first line of each column heading should range across the page. If an item in the first column has more than one line and is a 'title' which applies to items running across the table, those items should range on its first line. Where items in columns are in panel form, set items full left in column, ranging turns, and insert 3-pt. space between items. Turns in simple items 1 em (no extra space between items). Tables should not be spaced out to full measure, but set to give good spacing between columns, with a minimum of 1 em. (See pp. 157 and 158.)

Housing allowance (£)	College houses		Responsibility for rates	Arrangements about capital improvements
	Rent paid	College responsibility		
356	Nil	Major repairs and decorations	College	Paid by college
269	450, 490, 500, 170, 98, 360, 72, 140	External and major internal repairs	Part paid by college	Interest usually added to reduction
500	300, 360	Structural repairs; external decoration, materials for internal decorations	Fellow if rent paid; college otherwise	College, if of value to future occupants
50 for two fellows with vested interest	—	Maintenance and repairs	Rent free	No fixed policy

(*f*) The column contents, if unrelated, should range on the left with the column heading:

	Forest			
	Black	New	Sherwood	Speymouth
Age	20	43	35	69
Area sampled, acres	6.9	11.2	7.5	27.6
No. of trees	10,350	4,702	2,650	945
No. of infected trees	163	98	50	23
Infected trees, %	1.63	0.9	20.3	10.7
Chi-square for observed values	7.83	11.09	4.98	too small

If the contents are related, however, the longest item should range with the column heading and other items should range on the decimal point or comma:

Technique	Output	No. of workers	Output per man-year	Total wage-bill
I	34,200	4	12.2	225
II	45,968	10	7.4	364
III	9,732	2	4.7	198
IV	213,427	15	96.3	2,000
V	2,340,646	126	201.9	14,344

(*g*) Headlines should be inserted over full-page tables, whether set to text measure or turned sideways up page, unless the table area includes the space of the headline.

(*h*) For footnotes to tables the system of indices should be different from that used in the text, and the notes should be placed immediately below each table.

(*i*) Table titles are always to appear at the head of the table.

(*j*) Tables which extend on to two more pages:

(i) Column widths should remain constant on the continuation page(s), and column headings should be repeated on each page where tables read down the page. Insert a 'continued' line, e.g. 'Table 2 (*cont.*):', if table turns over to a left-hand page (not necessary if facing pages).

(ii) Where tables are turned sideways it is necessary to repeat column headings on the left-hand pages only. These tables should always be placed with the head on the left, whether on left- or right-hand pages.

(iii) A light rule should be used above repeated column headings (see (*c*) above).

(iv) Omit tail rules on each page until the table is completed.

THREE-LINE (AND LARGER) DROP INITIALS

Letters with a projecting left-hand stem should overhang into the margin (unless there are marginal notes or numbers immediately in front of the letter).

Examples:

THESE three divers general use in the have at least four although known in th is a solid derived chie industry was still in it

VIKINGS were kno especially in the f they had to use t areas in which they w succeeded by selectio opened up a phase in

WHETHER his fir but we can be he did not begi since it appears to be that could be employ either by using a new

YELLOW fields cha production of cro the other hand lat cultivation, once thou rapid growers must h shrubs and trees, and

And where J has a large bowl allow this to project into the margin:

> J APAN, a group of islan
> one and a half times th
> but twice the populatio
> in the earth's crust runs t
> of volcanoes and earthqua
> heavy monsoon rain in th

Where the initial is the first letter of a word avoid a gap between the initial and following letters by cutting the type to make a neat fit. The beginnings of the second and third lines should range clear of the initial.

Examples:

> A MONG the results o
> the long battle w
> in the prohibition
> protection against the
> uranium, for instance,
> for this purpose when

> L OCATED at well defi
> which break away
> the beginning of th
> colonies with few rings
> but his proposal for the
> which was in fact in us

If a quotation mark is required before a drop initial, it should be set in the margin in the same size as the text.

sticks, especially when Matthew Boulton and others introduced a technique for soldering-on silver thread to cover the copper exposed at the edges. A Birmingham invention was Muntz's metal (three parts of copper to two of zinc), which after 1832 replaced copper sheathing for the bottoms of ships in the merchant navy. Most kinds of brass, however, contained a higher proportion of copper, since it was prized for its handsome colour, resembling gold. Here, too,

FIG. 250. Making copper pigs, Lancashire, nineteenth century

Birmingham took the lead, and by 1795 was using a thousand tons a year. Gilt objects such as buttons were produced from what was called calamine brass, which was not a direct alloy of copper and zinc, but was obtained by heating copper together with calamine and charcoal. There was also much use of acids, dragon's blood (a kind of resin), and lacquer to vary or disguise the surface appearance of the many imitative wares for which Birmingham was becoming famous.

Chemical research was revealing the existence of new metals, but manufacturers on the whole were not very interested in developing their use, especially as extraction and working were often difficult: as late as 1828 S. F. Gray in *The Operative Chemist* contemptuously dismissed a number of them as mere hypothetical assumptions, adding his own opinion that 'nothing but the rage of the day for the invention of new metals could have prompted their

FIG. I

Owain which had developed from former *marcher*,
Denbigh near the castle and town, and Cliffwrn which
the lord had made out of escheated, or forfeited land.

Study carefully the plan of a typical English manor
below. Broadly it is divided into (a) the village and
lord's domain, (b) the three great tilled fields (each many
times the size of the average hedged field in Wales today)
all divided into roughly one-acre strips, (c) the grazing
meadow, and (d) the waste. The average manor in
Wales would not conform as closely to this pattern. The
Welsh countryside was too hilly and too broken by wood

36. A TYPICAL ENGLISH MANOR

Only the lord's land and the dwellings were permanently hedged. Temporary
hurdles, or brushwood fences, kept the animals off the meadows and the strips that
had other crops were harvested. Farmers and low banks alone separated the strips,
which were often mixed up in a most bewildering way. How can we tell, by studying
up a man's holding were not unified or fixed from year to year, but were scattered
over ... What the 'strath's that year are shaded. Can you suggest why? What
were the disadvantages?

THE TRIUMPH OF THE TUDORS 176

B: UPS AND DOWNS IN THE WARS OF THE ROSES

Not unlike a seismograph recording earthquakes, the graph shows the sudden
'shocks' of conflict and the bewildering changes of fortune of the war

By 1450, however, France had been lost, thanks mainly
to the mismanagement of the weak, saintly king, Henry
VI (1422-61). When in 1453 he became imbecile, the
right to govern in his place was claimed both by his master-
ful queen (for Lancaster) and by Richard of York. The
two sides gathered their armed forces, and, says an old
tale, their badges; a red rose for Lancaster and a white
for York. This war of the roses then began with the
First Battle of St. Albans in 1455, a victory for York.

The graph above shows that the war may broadly
be considered in six periods, three long periods of comparative quiet alternating with three short ones of furious
fighting.

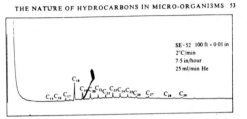

SE - 52   100 ft × 0·01 in
2°C/min
7·5 in/hour
25 ml/min He

C_{18}

C_{15} C_{16} C_{17} C_{19} C_{20} C_{21} C_{22} C_{23} C_{24} C_{25} C_{26} C_{27} C_{28} C_{29}

Fig. 3.13. Gas chromatogram of total alkanes from *Escherichia coli* (late log phase)

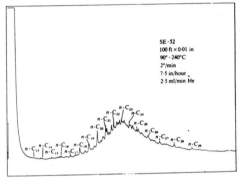

SE - 52
100 ft × 0·01 in
90° - 240°C
2°/min
7·5 in/hour
2·5 ml/min He

$n\text{-}C_{13}$ $n\text{-}C_{22}$ $n\text{-}C_{23}$ $n\text{-}C_{24}$
$n\text{-}C_{21}$
$n\text{-}C_{20}$ $n\text{-}C_{25}$
$n\text{-}C_{19}$ $n\text{-}C_{26}$
$n\text{-}C_{13}$ $n\text{-}C_{14}$ $n\text{-}C_{16}$ $n\text{-}C_{18}$ $n\text{-}C_{27}$ $n\text{-}C_{28}$ $n\text{-}C_{29}$
$n\text{-}C_{15}$ $n\text{-}C_{17}$

Fig. 3.14. Gas chromatogram of alkanes from yeast

hydrocarbons of higher molecular weight, around C_{34}, C_{35}, and C_{36} and
still higher, that were not apparent in the photosynthetic bacteria as a
major component of their hydrocarbon fraction. A striking example of
this difference is shown in Fig. 3.14, which is a gas chromatogram of the
alkanes from bakers' yeast. It exhibits a curious kind of distribution,
in which most of the peaks are in the C_{23} region. Because this shows such
a relatively smooth curve it is quite clear that there are many compounds
present that our chromatography has not yet succeeded in resolving.

FIG. 3

tend to collect in droplets. Further, an absorbent paper had to be used and, as absorption takes place both laterally and in depth, the result was an impression that was not only smudgy but showed through on the reverse side of the paper. Again, the viscosity of water is relatively low, so that the paper would tend to slide about on the surface of the block while the transfer of the ink was being effected by applying pressure; so further contributing to a poor impression.

Most of these difficulties were overcome by using an oil-bound ink, made by grinding boiled linseed-oil with lampblack or powdered charcoal. It is thought that the linseed-oil may have suggested itself through its use as a varnish by early fifteenth-century Flemish painters, and the discovery may have been applied to the inking of wooden blocks before the time of Gutenberg, to whom it has been generally attributed since 1499; in any event, the result was a standard ink employed for more than four centuries. Originally the pressure needed to transfer

FIG. 108. Printers at work, with type-cases and tympan, Frankfurt-am-Main, 1568

the ink from the block to the paper was achieved by rubbing the back of the paper with a leather pad; but a screw-press, with which greater and more uniform pressure could be attained, was soon substituted. For this, oil-bound ink was essential, since without it there would have been too great a risk of the paper moving during the operation.

The press was already familiar, being used, for example, in pressing linen and in paper-making, and required at first only slight modification for its new function. But the actual printing was considerably helped later by the introduction of the 'tympan', a parchment-covered frame to which the paper was fastened before printing. This was hinged in such a way as to bring the paper down exactly level with, and square to, the type (Fig. 108).

What has been said above applies to the origins of relief printing, with which the future lay, but the technique of intaglio printing—

FIG. 4

36. DOLBADARN CASTLE
Note the high peaks of Snowdonia
behind.
Copyright Roy. Comm. Anc. Mons.

where, it is said, he had been born. When later he built
Dolbadarn, guarding the pass of Llanberis, he followed
the new fashion in round keeps, while in building
Criccieth at the end of his reign he relied on a massive
gatehouse. At his castles and royal residences, especially
Aberffraw and Aber (near Bangor), he kept court and
met his officers and envoys, many of them churchmen.
The new feature of his period, however, was the growth
of a class of lay officials of state. Among them the
greatest was Ednyfed Fychan, who was his *distain*, or
steward, from 1215 onward, and whose family served the
princes of Gwynedd, Welsh and English, for the next two
hundred years. These new officials were rewarded by
grants of land and other privileges, and so became a
body of enterprising landowners, bound in loyalty and
self-interest to the prince rather than to a tribal-leader.
Agriculture, too, flourished as a result.

Llywelyn, also, it seems, revised the laws which bear
the name of his great predecessor, Hywel Dda, in order

FIG. 5

The origin of the distortion can be interpreted in terms of the Jahn–Teller effect even on a purely crystal-field theory, but the valence-bond (dsp^2 hybrids) and molecular-orbital descriptions with their insistence on the importance of covalence are probably more appropriate. 4-coplanar Cu^{2+} complexes are readily obtained.

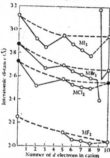

FIG. 24.20. Changes in interatomic distances in some MX_2 compounds of the first transition series. The points marked ● are estimates from ionic radii for 6-fold coordination of the cation

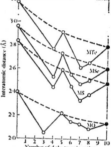

FIG. 24.21. Changes in interatomic distances in some MX compounds of the first transition series. The points marked ● are estimates from ionic radii for 6-fold coordination of the cation

In low-spin states bond distances are at least 0·1 Å shorter than in high-spin states. Unfortunately data are not available for a long series of comparable low-spin compounds. It is expected that the plots of distance against atomic number for the compounds of the second and third transition series (all low-spin) will go through a single minimum around perhaps the d^8 ions.

METAL-ION LIGAND DISTANCES IN COMPLEXES

A further simple test of the covalent polarization of ligands by cations is provided by interatomic distances in complexes. Covalent polarization will lead to bond-length contractions, and the more polarizable a ligand the greater will be this contraction. Generally nitrogen ligands are more polarizable than oxygen ligands, so that as a transition-metal series is

FIG. 6

Another instance is the male grayling's sexual pursuit flight. As was related above, dummies of females of different colours had about the same releasing value. There is, however, a slight difference. The darker

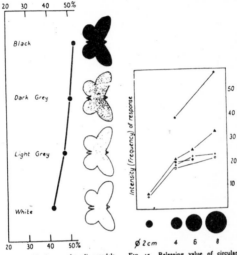

FIG. 44. Effectiveness of grayling models of various shades of grey. Changed after Tinbergen, Meeuse, Boerema, and Varossieau, 1942

FIG. 45. Releasing value of circular models of varying size as presented to male grayling. After Tinbergen, Meeuse, Boerema, and Varossieau, 1942

colours get more responses than the lighter ones. If models of different shades, varying from white to black, are presented, the darker shades get progressively more responses. A black model even evokes more reactions than a model in natural colours (Figs. 39, 44). Moreover, models of much greater size than normal get more responses than models of normal size (Fig. 45).

The full significance of the phenomenon of 'supernormal' sign stimuli is not yet clear. A closer study might well be worth while.

FIG. 7

bill was constant but the colour of the head was varied, showed that a model with a white head had no more releasing value than models with black, red, yellow, green, blue, &c., heads. These observations lead to the conclusion that the chick reacts especially to the red patch. This

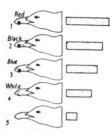

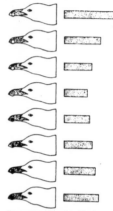

FIG. 22. Models of herring gull heads used to release begging responses in newly born chicks. Colour of the mandible. patch varied (1–4) or absent (5). Columns indicate relative frequency of chicks' responses. After Tinbergen, 1949

FIG. 23. Releasing value of herring gull models with grey bills with patches of varying shade. After Tinbergen, 1949

patch works through its colour and through its contrast with the colour of the bill.

No releasing value was found for either colour of the bill or colour of the head (Tinbergen, 1948*b*, 1949; Tinbergen and Perdeck, 1950).

The reactions of many birds to flying birds of prey are often released by quite harmless birds. The domestic cock gives its alarm call, not only when a sparrow hawk is passing, but also as a reaction to the sudden appearance of a pigeon or a crow. The special type of movement, the sudden appearance, is sufficient to elicit the alarm, although the shape of a pigeon is quite different from that of any bird of prey. In addition, many birds react to the typical shape of a bird of prey in flight. Heinroth and Heinroth (1928) relate how many birds in the Berlin zoo react by

FIG. 8

INDEX

NOTES

NOTES

NOTES

NOTES